From Struggles to Strength

Dr. Murli Dhar Dwivedy

Qurate
quratebooks.com

From Struggles to Strength
Dr. Murli Dhar Dwivedy

Published in 2025

© Published by

Qurate Books Pvt. Ltd.
Goa 403523, India
www.quratebooks.com
Tel: 1800-210-6527, Email: info@quratebooks.com

ISBN: 978-93-58984-08-8

1

A Journey to Dehradun: Madhav's Adventure and Growth

Dehradun, the capital of Uttarakhand, is renowned for its breathtaking landscapes, lush greenery, and serene ambiance. For Madhav, however, it wasn't just a picturesque city; it marked the start of an incredible journey that would shape his future.

The Big Move

Madhav lived with his family in a quaint village called Lahana, nestled in the Buxar district of Bihar. His father, a dedicated army officer, and his mother, a devoted homemaker, shared a common dream: to provide their children with the finest education possible. When they learned about the exceptional schools in Dehradun, they made a life-changing decision to relocate.

The news brought a mix of emotions for Madhav. Excitement danced in his eyes, but apprehension tugged at his heart—he had never ventured beyond the familiar boundaries of his village. With their belongings packed and hearts brimming with hope, the family embarked on their journey to Dehradun.

The train ride itself was an adventure. Madhav gazed in awe at the ever-changing scenery—expanses of green fields, shimmering rivers, and, finally, the majestic mountains. As the train wound its way into the hills, a cool, crisp breeze greeted them, hinting at the wonders that awaited.

For Madhav, stepping into Dehradun was like entering the pages of a fairy tale. The city, cradled by verdant hills, came alive with bustling markets and tranquil forests. It was a stark contrast to the simplicity of his village—a new world, vibrant and full of possibilities.

Settling In

Madhav's family moved into a government quarter located in the cantonment area, close to the heart of the city. The house came with a small garden, and from the portico, they could catch glimpses of the distant foothills—a view that seemed to whisper tales of adventure. Adjusting to the new environment was both challenging and exhilarating.

The family worked together as a team to set up their new home, turning the unfamiliar space into a warm and welcoming haven. Madhav's mother took charge of arranging the kitchen and bedrooms with meticulous care, while his father organized his study with precision. Madhav and his younger brother eagerly unpacked boxes, arranging their toys and books with a sense of ownership and excitement.

This move underscored the importance of teamwork and mutual support. Every challenge they faced was tackled together, with each family member contributing in their unique way. Madhav felt a profound sense of belonging as he realized that no matter where life took them, their unity as a family was their greatest strength.

An Excellent Neighbor

In Madhav's new neighborhood, there lived a family from Haryana—a kind and generous couple, Shri Abhay Singh Rana and his wife. Though they were just two in number, their warmth and goodwill were boundless.

Aunty, as everyone affectionately called her, had a heart of gold. She shared a close bond with Madhav's mother, and the two were inseparable, often seen laughing and chatting like lifelong friends. Aunty was not only a delightful conversationalist but also a culinary artist who loved experimenting with new dishes. She frequently invited Madhav and his younger brother over, treating them to delicious meals and even knitting them cozy sweaters.

Her kindness shone brightly during a difficult time when Madhav's mother fell seriously ill and had to be admitted to the military hospital for a week. Without hesitation, Aunty stepped in, preparing full meals for Madhav's family every single day during that challenging period. Her care was so heartfelt that it felt as though she was an extension of Madhav's family.

Aunty's nature was a blend of practicality, gentleness, and boundless generosity. Her soft-spoken demeanor and ever-present smile endeared her to everyone in the locality, earning her the respect and love of all her neighbors. She had an innate ability to sense when someone needed help and offered her support without waiting to be asked.

The bond between Madhav's family and Aunty's household grew so deep that it didn't feel like two separate families from different states of India—it felt like one united family, bound by love, respect, and mutual care. Aunty's presence was a blessing, and her selfless spirit left an indelible mark on Madhav's life.

A New School

Soon, it was time for Madhav to begin his school journey. He secured admission to Central School in Dehradun, renowned for its stellar academic achievements and vibrant extracurricular activities. Nestled in the serene hills and surrounded by lush greenery, the school offered an inspiring environment.

On his first day, Madhav was a mix of nerves and excitement. The thought of making new friends, exploring unknown horizons, and diving into new lessons filled him with anticipation. The school had a warm and welcoming atmosphere. The teachers were kind-hearted, and the students greeted him with friendliness.

Madhav quickly adapted to his new surroundings. He found the subjects fascinating, and the outdoor activities like rock climbing and nature walks were a refreshing change from his usual routine. The fresh mountain air and the breathtaking natural beauty around the school made both studying and playing feel like a privilege. Madhav's heart brimmed with happiness as he embraced this new chapter of his life.

Learning to Ride

One sunny afternoon, Madhav's cheerful uncle came to visit. Known for his knack for teaching kids new skills, he soon noticed that Madhav didn't know how to ride a bicycle. "It's time you learn!" his uncle declared enthusiastically.

They rented a bicycle from a nearby shop and headed to the local park. Madhav's uncle, with his encouraging smile, began the lesson. At first, Madhav struggled—balancing the bike felt impossible. He fell several times, each tumble leaving him with scraped knees and a bruised spirit.

But his uncle never wavered in his support. "You know," he said with a twinkle in his eye, "I fell so many times when I was learning that I lost count. But each fall was a step closer to mastering it." His stories of persistence and resilience inspired Madhav to keep trying.

Day by day, Madhav's confidence grew. And then, one magical moment, everything fell into place. He wobbled for a second, then steadied himself—and rode the bicycle without falling! A surge of joy and pride overwhelmed him.

The thrill of gliding through the park, the wind in his hair, and the realization that he had learned something new were unforgettable. Madhav had not only mastered the art of cycling but also discovered the power of perseverance and determination.

Overcoming Challenges

A New Journey Begins

Riding a bicycle was just the start of Madhav's adventure in Dehradun. The scenic yet hilly terrain presented its own set of challenges, demanding careful planning of his time and energy. On top of that, the schoolwork was far more demanding than what he had been accustomed to.

Balancing Act

As the days passed, Madhav began to feel overwhelmed. Balancing school, homework, and his desire to explore the vibrant city became a daunting task. Stress crept in, making it harder for him to enjoy his new surroundings.

A Father's Wisdom

Noticing his struggles, Madhav's father stepped in to guide him. He introduced Madhav to simple yet effective stress management techniques. They began with basic breathing exercises and meditation. Every morning, before school, the two would spend 15 peaceful minutes in the garden practicing mindfulness. This daily ritual helped Madhav calm his mind, regain focus, and approach his tasks with renewed clarity.

A Mother's Nurture

Madhav's mother also played a pivotal role in supporting him. She ensured the family had nutritious meals to maintain their energy and emphasized the importance of adequate rest. In the evenings, she would share inspiring stories about great personalities who overcame immense challenges. These tales of perseverance and resilience not only motivated Madhav but also instilled in him the strength to keep moving forward.

A New Outlook

With the combined support of his parents and the strategies he learned, Madhav began to embrace the challenges. The once-overwhelming schoolwork became manageable, and he even found time to explore the beautiful city of Dehradun. Slowly but surely, Madhav turned his struggles into stepping stones for personal growth.

The Joy of Family

Madhav's journey to Dehradun turned into an unexpected celebration of familial love and support. Each family member played a unique and irreplaceable role in his life. His brother was the ever-optimistic cheerleader, lifting his spirits during tough days. His mother's comforting meals and soothing presence made even the gloomiest days brighter, while his father's wisdom and guidance helped him navigate challenges with confidence.

Weekends were filled with laughter and adventure as the family ventured on picnics to the nearby hills. They would hike the serene trails, play games that filled the air with joy, and marvel at the breathtaking vistas of the mountains. These moments of togetherness became cherished memories, reminding Madhav of life's beauty and the irreplaceable bond of family.

Embracing a New Life

As the months rolled by, Madhav adapted to his new life in Dehradun. What initially seemed like an uphill battle transformed into an enriching experience. He made new friends at school who became his companions in this new chapter. His academic progress was remarkable, and he even mastered the art of riding his bicycle—a skill that had once seemed insurmountable.

The initial fears and struggles began to fade, replaced by resilience and self-confidence. Madhav realized the invaluable lessons his challenges had taught him: the strength of teamwork, the rewards of persistence, and the art of staying calm under pressure. Above all, he understood that the unwavering support of his family was his greatest asset, enabling him to overcome any obstacle.

A Bright Future

Madhav's journey was just the beginning of a promising future. The experiences and lessons from Dehradun became the foundation of his character and aspirations. He began dreaming of greater adventures, of exploring the world, and of making his family proud.

Standing on the porch one evening, watching the sun dip behind the majestic mountains, Madhav felt an overwhelming sense of gratitude. Dehradun, with its rolling hills, vibrant landscapes, and new experiences, had become his second home. It was here that he blossomed from a worried boy into a confident and capable young lad.

Lessons for a Lifetime

Madhav's adventure in Dehradun wasn't just about learning to ride a bicycle—it was a microcosm of life itself. It taught him to embrace challenges with determination, to adapt with flexibility, and to find joy in life's simple pleasures.

In the embrace of this beautiful city, surrounded by his loving family, Madhav discovered his true potential. He learned that life's hurdles, no matter how daunting, could be overcome with courage, persistence, and the unconditional love of those who matter most. His journey became a testament to growth, resilience, and the unyielding strength of family bonds.

"Challenges are not roadblocks; they are the stepping stones that shape your strength. Embrace them with determination, and you'll find the path to greatness."

2

Repairing the Canal: A Thought for the Welfare of the Community

In the quaint village of **Lahana**, nestled in the Buxar district of Bihar, life meandered at a leisurely pace. With a population of just about 350, the villagers shared a strong bond, knowing each other's names and supporting one another through joys and challenges. The village lacked proper roads, relying instead on dusty pathways that connected homes, fields, and the bustling marketplace. Two serene ponds, one to the east and the other to the north, mirrored the sun's glow, while a meandering canal to the west irrigated the fields that sustained the community.

The Stubborn Elder: Harsh Upadhyay

At the heart of this idyllic setting was **Harsh Upadhyay**, an elderly man who commanded attention in Lahana. His reputation wasn't just for his years but also for his fiery temper and failing eyesight. Armed with a stick, he often roamed the village, grumbling about the antics of the younger generation. His poor vision, worsened with age, limited his ability to see beyond a few meters. Yet, Upadhyay ji remained fiercely independent, stubbornly declining help from others, a trait that the villagers both admired and found frustrating.

Madhav: The Mischievous Prodigy

Among Lahana's children was **Madhav**, a 12-year-old boy with an unparalleled knack for mischief. Clever, quick-witted, and always brimming with energy, Madhav was a source of endless entertainment—and exasperation—for the villagers. His sharp mind often got him out of the trouble his pranks landed him in.

Madhav particularly enjoyed teasing Harsh Upadhyay, who was a frequent target of his jokes.

"**Madhav! You little rascal! Come back here!**" Upadhyay would bellow, waving his stick furiously, while Madhav darted away, his laughter echoing through the village lanes.

Despite the occasional scolding, the villagers secretly found Madhav's antics amusing. Whenever mischief occurred, the automatic assumption was, "It must be that boy, Madhav!" Even when innocent, he carried the blame with a grin that made it hard to stay mad at him.

The Bond Between Tradition and Youth

Though Madhav's pranks often left Harsh Upadhyay fuming, their exchanges brought a certain liveliness to Lahana. The old man's gruff reprimands and the boy's playful retorts highlighted the generational gap, yet also underscored the unique bond between tradition and youth in the village.

Harsh Upadhyay's stick-waving frustration and Madhav's irrepressible energy reflected the vibrant spirit of Lahana—a community where young and old coexisted in a tapestry of shared struggles, laughter, and mutual care.

The Broken Canal and Madhav's Plan

One sunny afternoon, Madhav and his friends sat under the sprawling banyan tree near the village pond, enjoying a brief respite from the day's chores. As they lounged, their attention was drawn to a group of elderly men deep in discussion.

"The canal to the west has broken," one man said with a sigh. "It's crucial for irrigating our crops, and without it, the fields are drying up." Another man shook his head grimly. "We'll have to wait for the district officials to come and fix it. But that could take weeks! By then, the crops will be ruined."

The words struck a chord with Madhav. He wasn't one to sit idly by, especially when faced with a challenge. His sharp mind quickly sparked an idea.

A Bold Proposition

"Why wait for officials when we can fix it ourselves?" Madhav declared, his eyes gleaming with determination. His friends stared at him in disbelief. "Fix the canal? Are you serious, Madhav? How can we do that?" Madhav grinned, his confidence unshaken. "We've seen the canal workers repair it before, haven't we? It's not impossible. All we need are tools, mud, and stones. If we work together, we can do it!"

For a moment, the boys hesitated. The idea seemed daunting. But Madhav's unwavering resolve was infectious. Slowly, they began to nod in agreement. It wasn't just a daring adventure—it was a chance to make a real difference.

The Boys Take Action

With newfound purpose, the boys gathered what they needed: shovels, baskets, and stones from the nearby fields. They made their way to the broken section of the canal, where water was spilling uncontrollably into the fields, creating a muddy mess.

At first, the task felt overwhelming. The break was wider than they'd anticipated, and the sun blazed down on them relentlessly. But Madhav quickly took charge.

"First, we need to block the water," he instructed. Grabbing a handful of stones, he began placing them strategically to redirect the flow. His friends followed his lead, and soon the water slowed enough for them to start repairing the damage.

An Afternoon of Hard Work

The boys worked tirelessly, their hands blistered from the rough stones and shovels. They dug mud from the sides of the canal, packed it tightly into the broken section, and reinforced it with stones.

Hours passed, and the sun began to dip toward the horizon, casting a warm golden glow over the fields. Exhausted, drenched in sweat, and covered in mud, the boys finally stepped back to admire their handiwork. The water, once spilling out uncontrollably, now flowed smoothly through the canal.

A Morning of Astonishment

The next morning, the villagers arrived to inspect the canal, fearing the worst. Instead, they were greeted by an incredible sight: the canal, fully repaired and functioning perfectly.

"Who did this?" one villager asked in astonishment. "It must have been the district workers," another speculated. But someone quickly pointed out, "They wouldn't have come this quickly."

Word soon spread that it was Madhav and his group of friends who had taken matters into their own hands. At first, the villagers were skeptical. Could a group of boys, led by the mischievous Madhav, have truly achieved this?

When the boys proudly confirmed their feat, the villagers were amazed.

Heroes of the Village

Madhav and his friends had proven that courage, teamwork, and determination could overcome even the most daunting challenges. The villagers showered them with praise and gratitude, and the boys, though tired, beamed with pride.

From that day on, Madhav was no longer seen as just a mischievous boy. He had shown the village what leadership and initiative could accomplish, inspiring everyone to believe in the power of collective effort.

Harsh Upadhyay, the elderly man who had often been the target of Madhav's pranks, was among the first to praise him. "That boy may be a troublemaker, but he's got a good heart," he said, shaking his head with a smile. "I always knew there was something special about him." The village buzzed with excitement. Madhav, the once mischievous prankster, had suddenly become a hero. The villagers, who had once scolded him for his tricks, now showered him with admiration. Even the village elders, who had often reprimanded him, couldn't stop talking about his cleverness and leadership.

For the first time, Madhav felt a sense of pride and responsibility. His sharp wit, once used for pranks and mischief, had now been harnessed to help his community. It was a lesson he would carry with him forever—that his intelligence and boundless energy could be channeled for good. From that day on, Madhav's reputation in the village transformed. He was still the same mischievous boy—after all, that was part of who he was—but now, the villagers saw him in a different light. He was no longer just the clever boy; they saw him as someone who truly cared about his village, someone who could rise to the occasion when needed.

For Madhav, this marked the beginning of a new chapter. No longer just the boy who teased Upadhyay ji, he was now Madhav—the boy who fixed the canal, the clever, resourceful, and compassionate young man who had earned the respect and praise of an entire village.

"Your life changes the moment you decide to stop waiting for the perfect moment and start creating it with every choice you make."

3

The Awakening of Madhav: A Tale of Tradition and Transformation

In the quaint village of Lahna, age-old traditions are lovingly preserved, passing down from generation to generation. Every February, the village comes alive with anticipation for the cultural programs and the grand Saraswati Puja. This festival, dedicated to the Hindu goddess of music, arts, and knowledge, holds great significance, especially for the young students of the village. For those preparing for their board exams in class XI, it is a time to shine, seek blessings for their academic pursuits, and showcase their talents before the entire village. This year, the festival holds a special meaning for Madhav, a quiet and introspective 15-year-old boy.

Madhav's Quiet Struggles

Madhav had always been known for his shyness and hesitation. He was often seen as an outsider among his peers, someone who preferred to remain in the background. But deep within, Madhav harbored a well of creativity and a strong desire to step out of the shadows. When the village elders called for volunteers to organize the Saraswati Puja, Madhav felt an inexplicable but compelling urge to rise to the occasion. With nervous excitement, he approached his friends with a proposal: "This year, we should organize a grand play to be the main attraction of the festival." The idea was met with mixed reactions of skepticism and enthusiasm.

The Challenge Ahead

Baban, a brilliant and articulate boy, was the first to voice his doubt. "We've never done something like this before. And Madhav, you've never faced a crowd. How can we possibly do this?" Madhav, though anxious, accepted the challenge with quiet determination. His voice was barely above a whisper, but there was resolve in his words. "I know this is a big challenge," he said, "But I believe that together, we can make it happen. We just need to work together." His sincerity and quiet confidence slowly began to win over his classmates.

A Team Formed

Impressed by Madhav's newfound determination, Baban agreed to help. Together, they formed a team of eight students, each contributing their unique strengths. Rajesh, a talented artist, took charge of designing the sets; Priya, with her melodious voice, was entrusted with enhancing the music; and Ravi, with his passion for writing, took on the task of scripting the play. Others eagerly joined in, contributing ideas, costumes, and energy to the rehearsals.

Lessons in Leadership

Madhav, though still overwhelmed, found himself shouldering many responsibilities. He coordinated with the team, sought donations from villagers, and ensured every detail was meticulously planned. Each day brought lessons in overcoming his natural shyness and hesitation. There were moments of doubt when he questioned his ability to lead, and whether the play would live up to the expectations of the village. One such moment came during a crucial rehearsal when tensions ran high. The actors' delivery was off, and the atmosphere was one of despair. Madhav felt a deep wave of doubt, but he knew he had to push forward.

The Turning Point

Taking a deep breath, Madhav walked forward and clapped his hands to get everyone's attention. His voice, steady but firm, cut through the tension. "I know it's tough. I know we're all nervous. But we need to focus. This program is for the entire village. We all have a chance to create something beautiful—something that will be remembered for years to come. Let's work together and make it successful." His words had a transformative effect on the team. With renewed energy, they refocused and practiced with enthusiasm and sincerity, something that had been lacking earlier.

A Moment of Triumph

As the day of Saraswati Puja approached, the excitement in Lahna grew. Whispers of the grand drama spread through the village, and the villagers became curious about the preparations the young students had made. A temporary stage was set up at the village school, decorated with colorful ornaments, adding to the festive atmosphere. On the night of the performance, Madhav stood backstage, his heart pounding in his chest. Despite weeks of preparation, his shyness began to resurface.

Facing the Fear

Sensing his unease, Baban placed a reassuring hand on Madhav's shoulder and smiled warmly. "Everyone trusts you, Madhav. Now go out there and show everyone what we've worked so hard to create." Madhav took a deep breath and stepped forward, the curtains rising in front of a cheering crowd. As he walked onto the stage, his initial fear melted away, replaced by the pride of seeing his work come to life.

The Grand Performance

The play unfolded beautifully. Each scene was a testament to the hard work and dedication of the students. The villagers, mesmerized by the performance, watched with awe as the young actors and crew showcased their talents. The final scene brought the play to a powerful conclusion, and as the curtain fell, the crowd erupted in thunderous applause. Madhav and his team stood together, basking in the glow of their success.

The Transformation

In that moment, Madhav realized that the performance was more than just a play. It was a celebration of the collective effort, a reminder of the power of unity, and the strength that comes from believing in oneself. His heart swelled with gratitude as tears welled in his eyes. He had not only led his peers to create something extraordinary, but he had also discovered a newfound sense of confidence and purpose. The shy, hesitant boy had transformed into a capable leader.

A Historic Saraswati Puja

That year's Saraswati Puja became a historic event in Lahna. The play was remembered not only for its grandeur but also for the inspirational journey of Madhav. The young boy who dared to step out of his comfort zone had led his peers to create something truly remarkable. When the village celebrated the success of the festival, Madhav couldn't help but feel a deep sense of joy and fulfillment, knowing that he had found his voice and his place in the world.

"Transformation begins the moment you decide to shed your fears and embrace the possibilities. Every change, no matter how small, is a step towards the person you're meant to be."

4

Madhav's Journey to Roorkee

Madhav, a boy from Lahna village, was known for his mischievous nature and sharp intelligence. However, he was also notorious for his lack of focus on studies. His father, who served in the army, was often away. Madhav's mother and the rest of the family were deeply concerned about his future. After much deliberation, they decided to send him to Roorkee, a city in the Saharanpur district of Uttar Pradesh, in search of better educational opportunities.

The Decision to Move

Madhav's family believed that a structured environment at a good school in Roorkee would help him focus on his studies. His father, too, was part of this decision. One evening, he called Madhav over to explain the plan. "To build your future, you need to focus on your studies," his father said. He continued, "We've decided to send you to Roorkee for better education. You'll stay with your uncle and study in a good school there."

Though Madhav was apprehensive about leaving his home and friends, he understood the significance of this change. With a mixture of fear and determination, he nodded silently, knowing that this move could shape his future.

The Challenge of the Migration Certificate

Before Madhav could join the school in Roorkee, there was one crucial task: obtaining his migration certificate. One rainy morning, his father asked him to collect the certificate from the district office. The importance of this document weighed heavily on Madhav's mind. The task had to be completed that day itself.

Madhav's heart sank. He was always afraid of going to new places alone, and the thought of venturing to the district office in such weather filled him with dread. However, not wanting to disappoint his father, he mustered the courage to go.

The Trip to the Office

As soon as Madhav stepped outside, the rain poured down relentlessly. His clothes quickly became soaked, and the roads turned into rivers of water. He walked carefully, holding an umbrella, though it offered little protection from the rainstorm. The journey was long and treacherous. Madhav slipped several times, his shoes scraping against the wet pavement with each step.

Despite the discomfort and his fear, he pressed on, inspired by the thought of his father's faith in him. The road seemed endless, but Madhav didn't stop.

Overcoming Language Barriers

When Madhav finally reached the district office, another challenge awaited him: the language barrier. The officials spoke in formal Hindi, which Madhav struggled to understand. Nervously, he approached one of the officials to explain his purpose.

"I need to get my migration certificate," Madhav said, his voice trembling slightly. The official, engrossed in his paperwork, barely glanced at him and asked for the name of the school. Feeling the pressure mounting, Madhav hesitated before responding, "Sir, the school is in Roorkee. My father is in the army, and I need to join a new school there."

Seeing the fear and determination in Madhav's eyes, the man finally looked up. Softening a little, he gave Madhav clear instructions on where to go and whom to speak to.

Courage and Leadership

Following the instructions, Madhav found the correct office. Inside, the clerk was busy, and a long line of people waited. Madhav took a deep breath and reminded himself of the importance of his task. As he stood in the queue, he noticed the chaos around him—people arguing and pushing forward.

Despite his fear, Madhav decided to take charge. With surprising confidence, he spoke up, "Everyone has important work here. We should all stand in line, and as our turn comes, we'll get our work done."

To his surprise, the crowd listened. People began organizing themselves, forming an orderly line. The clerk, noticing this change, smiled at Madhav. His courage and leadership had not only helped him navigate a difficult situation but had also made a difference in the chaotic environment of the office.

Collecting the Certificates

When his turn came, Madhav approached the clerk and explained his situation. The clerk nodded, checked his records, and handed over the migration certificate.

"Good work, young man," said the clerk with a smile. "You showed great leadership there. Your father would be proud."

Madhav's heart swelled with pride and relief. He thanked the clerk and carefully placed the certificate in his bag. The journey back home was as challenging as the one to the office. The rain had not stopped, and the roads had become even more dangerous. But this time, Madhav felt a new courage. He had faced his fear and succeeded.

As he walked, he thought about his father and the new life waiting for him in Roorkee. A mixture of emotions filled him—fear of the unknown, sadness at leaving his home, and excitement about the new opportunities ahead.

Arrival in Roorkee

A week later, Madhav found himself in Roorkee. The city buzzed with activity, and everything felt strange and overwhelming. His uncle welcomed him warmly, making him feel at ease in the unfamiliar surroundings.

The school in Roorkee was large and well-organized. On his first day, Madhav felt out of place among the confident city kids, but he reminded himself of the courage he had shown while collecting the migration certificate.

Adapting to the New Environment

Madhav faced several challenges at his new school. The curriculum was more advanced, and the teachers were strict. He struggled with the language and the pace of lessons. But every time he felt defeated, he remembered his father's words and the determination that had carried him through the rainy day at the court.

Madhav decided to dedicate extra hours to studying, seeking help from his teachers and classmates. His intelligence, combined with newfound focus, helped him catch up quickly. Slowly, the new environment began to feel less intimidating.

Building Friendships

Despite his initial struggles, Madhav started to make friends. His classmates admired his dedication and willingness to help others. He became known for his leadership qualities, organizing study groups, and offering help with difficult subjects.

One day, the school organized a cultural event. Madhav, though initially hesitant, decided to participate. He performed a traditional dance from his village, showcasing his roots and impressing everyone with his talent.

The event was a turning point for Madhav. He gained confidence and a sense of belonging. His teachers and classmates began to see him not just as a new student, but as a valuable member of their community.

The Unwavering Support of His Father

Throughout Madhav's journey, his father remained a constant pillar of support. They stayed in regular communication, and his father's encouraging words kept him motivated. "Madhav, I am so proud of you," his father would say during their calls. "You've shown incredible courage and determination. Keep going, and you will accomplish great things."

The Path to a Peaceful Life

As months passed, Madhav's hard work began to bear fruit. He excelled in his studies, earning top grades and receiving praise from his teachers. His leadership abilities flourished, and he became a respected figure among his peers. The village, hearing of his success, took immense pride in his achievements. Madhav became an inspiration to other children, showing them that with courage and determination, they too could overcome challenges and reach for their dreams.

Life in Roorkee settled into a peaceful rhythm. Madhav found a balance between his academic responsibilities and extracurricular activities, forming lasting friendships while building a bright future for himself.

Reflecting on His Journey

Looking back, Madhav realized that the journey to the District office on that rainy day had been a defining moment in his life. It had taught him invaluable lessons about courage, leadership, and perseverance. He had faced his fears head-on and emerged stronger. His family, especially his father, were proud of the man he had become. Madhav knew that he had made them proud and was determined to continue growing and succeeding on his path.

Conclusion: A Story of Courage, Determination, and Growth

Madhav's story is one of transformation—of courage, resilience, and personal growth. From a timid boy who struggled to focus on his studies, he evolved into a confident, responsible young man ready to take on the world. His journey was filled with challenges, but with the support of his family and his own inner strength, he overcame every obstacle.

In the peaceful city of Roorkee, surrounded by supportive friends and family, Madhav discovered not just education, but a sense of purpose and belonging. His story is a powerful reminder that with courage, determination, and the support of those around us, we can conquer any challenge and build a fulfilling life.

"Education is the key that unlocks the doors to endless possibilities. With every lesson learned, you pave the way to a future filled with growth, opportunity, and success."

5

The Uncertain Journey

Madhav's father had been posted in Amritsar, Punjab, and had come to Roorkee for a day to ensure that his family was settled properly. As he was preparing to return to Amritsar, he told Madhav, "I'm leaving your mother and sister at Ganeshpur. You need to go to BSM College. There, you will meet a man named Mr. Rakkam Singh. He will guide you through the admission process. Don't worry, everything will be fine." Madhav nodded, but his throat went dry. The thought of traveling alone to an unknown city, without his father's presence, terrified him. He watched as his mother and sister bid him farewell and disappeared into the busy streets of Ganeshpur. His father dropped him at the gates of BSM College. Madhav felt a surge of nervousness. He felt completely alone and unsafe.

The Encounter with Mr. Singh

Madhav entered the college campus with hesitant steps. The sounds of students chatting, the ringing of bells, and the occasional teacher's voice echoed around him, intensifying his anxiety. He spotted a sign pointing to the administration office and walked towards it, hoping to find Mr. Rakkam Singh. The office was small and cluttered, with shelves full of dusty files and an old ceiling fan whirring above. Behind a chaotic desk sat a man in his forties, wearing thick glasses and a neatly pressed shirt. Madhav assumed this was Shri Rakkam Singh. "I've come for admission in class 10th. My father has sent me to you," Madhav said nervously. Mr. Singh looked up from his papers, studying Madhav through the lenses of his glasses. His expression was unreadable, which only heightened Madhav's unease. "You'll need to meet the principal," Mr. Singh said in a neutral tone. "He will decide about your admission. His office is down the hall, third door on the left." Madhav's heart sank. Meeting the principal felt like an overwhelming task. His legs grew heavy as he walked down the hall, his fear intensifying with every step. What if the principal didn't like him? What if he failed the exam? These thoughts swirled in his mind.

Facing the Principal

The door to the principal's office was solid wood, polished to a high sheen. Standing before it, Madhav felt dwarfed by the imposing figure of the door. Trying to steady his nerves, he took a deep breath and knocked softly. The office was vast, with afternoon sunlight streaming through large windows. Behind a massive desk sat the principal—tall, imposing, with a stern face and sharp, calculating eyes. He looked up from his papers, his gaze locking with Madhav's. "Why have you come here?" The principal's voice carried an air of authority. Madhav stammered, his voice trembling, "I... I need admission in class 10th. Mr. Rakkam Singh sent me to you." The principal studied him for a long moment, his expression unreadable. Madhav's heart raced, his palms slick with sweat. Finally, the principal spoke again, his tone firm. "Admission to class 10th is not easy. We only admit students who are serious about their studies. You will need to pass a test to prove that you are capable. Be here tomorrow morning at 9 AM sharp. Do not be late." Madhav nodded quickly. The principal's strict demeanor left no room for discussion. With a heavy heart, Madhav exited the office, the weight of uncertainty pressing down on him as he faced the unknown challenges ahead.

The Test of Nerves

That night, Madhav found it difficult to sleep. His mind was overwhelmed with thoughts of the upcoming examination. What if the test didn't go well? What if he disappointed his father? The fear of failure haunted him. He lay awake, staring at the ceiling, until the early hours of the morning. When he finally drifted off, his dreams were filled with math problems and impossible questions.

He woke up before dawn, feeling tired but determined. He couldn't allow his fear to take control. Madhav arrived at the college early, and the eerie silence of the campus in the soft morning light made his nerves jitter even more. Standing outside the principal's office, his heart pounded. When the principal finally arrived, Madhav stood up, his heart racing in his chest.

The principal smiled and said, "It's good to see you here on time." As he handed over the test paper, he explained that Madhav had one hour to complete it, and all questions were compulsory.

Madhav took the exam paper with trembling hands. The questions stared back at him. Eight were related to mathematics, and two were on general knowledge. Mathematics was Madhav's favorite subject, and his mood lightened a little. He took a deep breath and focused all his energy on the task at hand.

The math problems were challenging but not impossible. Madhav found himself falling into a rhythm as he solved each question. His mind raced as he worked through the problems, and even the general knowledge questions, though requiring more thought, were manageable. Time seemed to fly by, and before he knew it, the hour was up.

He handed the paper back to the principal, who took it silently. The next few minutes felt like hours as the principal read through the answers, marking them with a red pen. Finally, he looked up with an unreadable expression.

"The answers to all the questions are correct," he said. "You've scored 50 out of 50. You can join college starting tomorrow."

Madhav sighed in relief. The fear that had plagued him for so long began to fade away. He was overjoyed. His first instinct was to share the news with his parents. Both were thrilled, their faces lighting up with pride.

The New Beginning

The next day, Madhav stood at the gates of BSM College, filled with mixed emotions. Although the fear still lingered, a new sense of courage had started to grow within him. He knew the road ahead would be challenging, but he was ready to face it.

As he walked through the campus, he saw students chatting with friends, hurrying to class, and laughing together. College no longer seemed like a scary place. It was a new beginning – a chance to grow, learn, and prove himself.

He entered his classroom, where the teachers were already writing on the blackboard. The room buzzed with the chatter of students, some of whom looked at him curiously. Madhav chose an empty seat at the back.

Though he still felt nervous, he pushed the feeling aside. He was here to learn, and nothing would distract him from that goal. As the lesson began, Madhav slowly started to settle in. The teachers were strict but fair, and the subjects were challenging but engaging.

With each passing day, his confidence grew. His fear was replaced by curiosity and excitement.

A Growing Confidence

As weeks turned into months, Madhav started to enjoy his time at college. He made many new friends and became more involved in class discussions. He even joined the math club, where he discovered his passion for solving complex problems.

Madhav also began to appreciate the city of Roorkee. At first, it had seemed disorganized and intimidating, but now, he was starting to see its charm. He visited the nearby Ganga canal with his new friends, and the city slowly became a part of him, just as the college did.

His relationship with his father also improved. When his father saw Madhav's progress, he was overjoyed. He realized that the fear he had seen in Madhav was not weakness, but rather the courage to face new challenges. As they shared stories of their days, their bond grew stronger. Madhav found a mentor and a friend in his father.

Facing New Challenges

The end of the academic year brought new challenges. Madhav's final exams were approaching, and the pressure was increasing. He studied for long hours, sometimes continuing until late at night. The fear of failure resurfaced, but this time, it was different. Madhav had learned to manage his fears. Instead of considering himself helpless, he had learned to use fear as inspiration. On the day of the final exam, Madhav felt uncomfortable. But as he sat in the examination hall surrounded by his classmates, he felt a sense of peace. He knew that he had prepared well, and no matter the outcome, he had given his best. When the results were announced, Madhav's heart started beating faster as he looked at the list. His name was among the top scorers. A wave of relief and pride washed over him. He not only passed but also excelled.

The Future Beckons

Madhav stood at the gates of BSM College one last time, a year after he had first arrived. The college had become a second home to him, a place where he had learned not just academics but also life lessons. As he looked back at the building that had once seemed so threatening, he felt a deep sense of gratitude. He knew that the future was still full of worries, and there would be new challenges and new fears to face. But he was no longer fearful.

"Your potential is limitless; it's not the obstacles that define you, but the courage you summon to overcome them. Keep pushing forward, and greatness will follow."

6

Madhav's First Day: A Test of Character

A New Beginning

Today was Madhav's first day at BSM College, and he was about to step into a classroom full of strangers. The excitement of passing the entrance exam quickly gave way to a new worry—the unfamiliarity of it all. A new city, a new school, and a sea of new faces surrounded him. The thought of entering a classroom where he knew no one except the principal and Mr. Rakam Singh made him uneasy. As he walked through the halls, the weight of being the new kid pressed heavily on him.

His first two periods passed quietly. Madhav was a listener, more focused on absorbing his surroundings than participating. The other students, already familiar with each other, chatted and laughed, making Madhav feel like an outsider. He reminded himself, however, that he had come here to excel in his studies and to make his family proud.

The Mathematics Lesson

The third period was Mathematics, a subjectMadhav loved. He was curious to see how it would be taught in this new environment. As soon as he entered the classroom, he sensed a shift in the students' energy. They seemed more restless, whispering among themselves as they settled into their seats.

The mathematics teacher, Shri Verma, a bespectacled man in his forties with a calm demeanor, entered the room. He greeted the class with a firm "Good morning." His voice carried a sense of authority, but the students responded with grumbles. Madhav noticed the lack of respect in their tone. Shri Verma sat down at his desk, focused on the blackboard, and immediately began writing.

The Problem on the Board

Shri Verma wrote a complex quadratic equation on the board. Madhav's eyes lit up. He enjoyed these kinds of challenges. He watched intently as the teacher began explaining the steps to solve it. But as Shri Verma wrote the solution on the board, the students started whispering among themselves. Some of them even laughed. Madhav felt a strange tension in the room but kept his attention on the board.

After solving the equation, Shri Verma turned towards the class and discussed alternative methods for solving the problem. For a moment, the room fell silent. Then, a few students stood up. One of them loudly complained, "The solution to this problem is too difficult! You're making it more complicated than it needs to be." Another student chimed in, saying they didn't understand his methods and perhaps needed a different teacher.

A Shocking Rebellion

Madhav was stunned by the students' audacity. He looked at Shri Verma, who remained calm, but there was a visible weariness in his eyes. It was clear that this was not the first time students had protested in such a manner. The complaints grew louder, and some students began questioning the teacher's qualifications. The room descended into chaos as the students openly rebelled against their teacher's methods. Madhav, shocked and surprised, couldn't believe what he was witnessing.

The Principal Intervenes

As the noise in the classroom escalated, the matter eventually reached the principal's office. After a while, the principal walked in, and the students quickly returned to their seats, the room falling nearly silent. However, a few students continued whispering among themselves. The principal's gaze scanned the room, his presence commanding attention. With a calm yet firm voice, he asked the students what the disturbance was about.

Shri Verma sighed, then pointed to the blackboard, explaining that he had been trying to solve a problem when the students began complaining about the difficulty of the lesson. The principal turned to the class and asked if any student found the problem easy to understand. An uncomfortable silence followed. The students, once so vocal, now avoided the principal's gaze. His eyes eventually landed on Madhav, who had been quietly observing the situation. The principal, sensing Madhav's presence, asked him what he thought, given that he was new to the class.

Madhav's Courage

Madhav took a deep breath. He could feel the weight of the situation — the expectations of both the teacher and the principal, and the piercing gazes of his classmates. But more than anything, he felt a sense of responsibility to speak the truth, regardless of the consequences. With a steady voice, Madhav began, "This problem can actually be solved in three different ways. Shri Verma's method is one of them."

The principal raised an eyebrow, clearly intrigued. "Would you be willing to explain all three methods on the board?" he asked.

Madhav hesitated for a moment. Solving problems in his head was one thing, but explaining them to the entire class was another, especially in such a tense environment. But then he remembered his father's words about courage and facing challenges head-on. This was his moment to prove himself.

With newfound determination, Madhav stood up from his seat. "Yes, I can explain them on the board," he replied confidently.

The Black Board Challenge

Madhav walked to the front of the class, his heart racing, but his mind focused. The eyes of the entire class were on him, their attention now fully captured. He took the chalk from Shri Verma and began writing on the blackboard. Madhav started by explaining the method used by Shri Verma, carefully walking the class through each step. As he spoke, the students grew more engaged, their attention fixed on him.

Once Madhav finished explaining the first method, he asked, "Does anyone have any questions?"

When no one responded, he moved on to the second method. This approach involved a step-by-step analysis, which Madhav presented clearly and methodically. The room remained quiet as the students followed along, some even nodding in understanding.

Finally, Madhav demonstrated the third method, the simplest of the three, which he had learned in his previous school. By the time he finished, the board was filled with equations, each method clearly outlined. Madhav stepped back, handing the chalk to Shri Verma. "These are the three ways," he said.

The Principal's Praise

The principal nodded in approval. He turned to the class and said, "Madhav has not only demonstrated his understanding of the problem, but he has also shown his ability to communicate it effectively to all of you." The principal's voice softened as he added, "I hope you all learn from his example."

The students looked down, some feeling embarrassed, others deep in thought. The principal's words lingered in the air, leaving a lasting impact on the entire class.

A Lesson in Respect

The principal stepped out of the room, heading toward his office. The tension that had gripped the class started to dissolve. Shri Verma, who had been silent until now, praised Madhav for his exceptional performance. There was a genuine tone of gratitude in his voice as he acknowledged Madhav's efforts. Madhav nodded modestly and returned to his seat. The rest of the class continued without incident. Shri Verma resumed his teaching, and the students quickly became engrossed in their work. When the period ended, some students approached Madhav. A few boys showered him with praise, while others playfully remarked, "Madhav is Bihari—Biharis are good at mathematics!" Madhav smiled, relieved that the situation had taken a positive turn.

Madhav shared with them that mathematics had always been his favorite subject. The group of students nodded in agreement, their initial reservations about him starting to fade away. One of the boys invited him to join them for lunch, marking a moment of acceptance for Madhav. It was a crucial step toward adjusting to his new school.

Newfound Confidence

Over the next few weeks, Madhav gradually adapted to his new environment. The incident in the mathematics class had earned him a reputation—not just as a brilliant student, but also as someone who was both courageous and principled. He noticed that more and more students began to approach him as a friend. Even the teachers, including Mr. Verma, began to recognize his potential. However, more importantly, Madhav had learned a valuable lesson. The challenging situation in the math class had given him an opportunity to demonstrate his skills and to stand by what he believed was right.

He realized that true courage isn't just about confronting others—it's about maintaining integrity and focus, even in the face of adversity. As the months passed, Madhav continued to excel academically, and the school environment, which had once felt discouraging, became a place where he felt he truly belonged. His newfound confidence and flexibility helped him both understand his studies better and navigate the social dynamics of school life.

The Nuisance Turned Ally

One day, during a break, Madhav was in the library, reading a book on advanced mathematical principles. Suddenly, a voice called out to him—one that he recognized. It was the same student who had been the most vocal during the protest in the math class, the one who had complained that Shri Verma was unsuitable for teaching. The student, Rohit, asked if he could sit next to Madhav.

Madhav smiled and nodded. Rohit sat down and thanked him, explaining that mathematics had always been difficult for him. "The way you explained things in Shri Verma's class that day made me realize that I've been approaching it all wrong," Rohit confessed. Madhav was surprised, but also pleased. He assured Rohit that while math could be tough, it was not impossible. "Sometimes, you just need to look at it from a different perspective," Madhav said. "If you ever need help, I'd be happy to discuss your problems with you."

Rohit smiled, and the tension that had once existed between them melted away. As they talked, Madhav discovered that Rohit, despite his rebellious nature, wasn't so different from him. They both had their struggles; while Madhav found solace in focusing on his studies, Rohit had channeled his frustrations into defiance. Over time, Rohit became one of Madhav's closest friends, and their relationship became a testament to the power of understanding and mutual respect.

The Power of Simplicity and Focus

As time passed, Madhav continued to shine not just in mathematics, but in all subjects. He was known for his simplicity, focus, and willingness to help others. He never flaunted his intelligence. Even the students who had once been notorious for creating trouble began to change. The overall school environment began to improve. There were still occasional pranks, but the respect for teachers and for learning grew stronger.

Madhav's relationship with Shri Verma deepened as well. He would often stay after class to discuss complex problems, and Shri Verma would challenge him with riddles that stretched his thinking further. Throughout all of this, Madhav remained humble. He knew his journey had only just begun, and that there would be many more challenges ahead.

But the most important lesson he learned was that even the toughest problems could be solved with focus, resourcefulness, and honesty.

A Journey of Courage and Belonging

As the school year came to an end, Madhav reflected on his first day at BSM College with a smile. The fear and uncertainty that had once weighed him down had given way to confidence and a deep sense of belonging. He had faced the unknown, navigated the chaos, and emerged stronger. Standing at the school gate, ready to head home for the holidays, Madhav knew that whatever challenges the future held, he would face them with the same courage and determination that had helped him succeed on that very first day in mathematics class.

"Believe in your journey, for every step, no matter how small, brings you closer to the greatness within you."

7

Journey to Haridwar by Bicycle

On a bright Saturday morning at 6 am, Madhav and his five friends decided to embark on an adventurous bicycle trip to Haridwar. The idea had come up spontaneously during a conversation about the discovery of the city, and the group was buzzing with excitement. Haridwar, a city of great spiritual significance, was only two hours away by bicycle. The boys were eager to visit the famous Har Ki Pauri and enjoy a picnic on the banks of the Ganges. As the first rays of the sun barely lit up the horizon, the group gathered at Madhav's house, each one carrying a small bag with essentials - snacks, water bottles, and a change of clothes. The crisp morning breeze filled them with energy as they saddled up and began their journey.

The Journey Begins

The road to Haridwar was a mix of smooth slopes and occasional uphill stretches. The boys, however, were so caught up in their excitement that they hardly noticed the slight inconvenience of the terrain. They chatted, laughed, and competed with one another, their spirits soaring. Madhav, being the most focused of the group, reminded everyone to stick together and watch out for traffic. Safety was important, but so was having fun. As they neared Haridwar, the road became more crowded with pilgrims and tourists heading to the holy city. The boys rode through the busy streets, exhilarated by the thought of reaching their destination.

Reaching Haridwar

When the group finally reached Har Ki Pauri, the iconic ghat on the banks of the Ganges, the sight of the river shimmering in the early morning light left them speechless. Madhav quickly secured his bicycle and, without wasting any time, rushed into the river. The cold water sent shivers down his spine, but it felt refreshing. The boys splashed around, laughing and enjoying the holy dip, feeling both happy and blessed in this sacred place. Afterward, they changed into fresh clothes and headed to a small eatery near the ghat to have breakfast. The puri-sabzi and lassi were absolutely delicious, fueling them for the rest of their exploration.

A Spiritual Journey

The boys then visited several temples, each one more awe-inspiring than the last. They marveled at the intricate architecture and soaked in the spiritual atmosphere. Each temple had its own unique story, and the boys spent their time praying, exploring, and enjoying the serenity of the place.

The Missing Shoe and Unexpected Trouble

However, their joyful day took an unexpected turn when they exited one of the temples. Madhav was shocked to see that one of his friend's shoes, Arjun's, was missing. Arjun, visibly upset, explained that his father had bought him new shoes just two days ago, and he couldn't believe someone had stolen them. The boys quickly spread out to search the area for any clues. Just as they were about to give up, a commotion broke out nearby. People had spotted a man running away with the shoes, and a crowd had gathered to catch him. The boys rushed over, relieved to see that the thief had been caught. Arjun recognized his shoes in the man's hand, and they were returned to him.

The Police Intervention

Just when things seemed to calm down, the police arrived. The officers interrogated the thief, who eventually confessed to the theft and handed over the shoes. The police warned the boys to be more cautious in crowded areas and advised them to stay together at all times. Though the incident had cast a shadow over their otherwise perfect day, it had a silver lining. The group became more united, realizing the importance of looking out for one another, especially in busy and unfamiliar places.

The Return Journey and Challenges

After returning the shoes to Arjun, the boys decided to head back to Roorkee. Kamlesh suggested they stop for some ice cream, and everyone agreed it was a great idea. Kamlesh found a nearby vendor, and they enjoyed the cool, creamy dessert, which lifted their spirits. With a renewed sense of energy, they resumed their journey, the mood light and the boys full of laughter, reminiscing about the day's events, including the shoe incident.

But the adventure was far from over. About halfway to Roorkee, Madhav heard a loud, strange sound and felt his bicycle wobble. He immediately swerved, signaling the others to follow him. As he inspected his tire, he quickly announced that it was punctured. Stranded in the middle of nowhere with no repair shops nearby, the boys exchanged worried glances, realizing they would have to work together to solve the problem and continue their journey.

Teamwork in Action

Rohit, who had a knack for mechanics, took charge. "Let's see if anyone has a repair kit," he suggested. Fortunately, Kamlesh had brought one along for emergencies. The boys worked together to remove the wheel, locate the puncture, and fix it. The process was challenging, especially under the hot afternoon sun, but the boys remained determined. They joked and kept their spirits high, turning the challenge into a team-building exercise rather than a setback. Madhav, always the leader, encouraged everyone to stay focused and positive. In less than half an hour, the tire was fixed, and they were back on the road.

The Final Stretch and a New Bond

With the tire repaired, the boys set off once more. The sun was now lower in the sky, and the journey became more tiring. The initial excitement had worn off, and fatigue began to set in. But with thoughts of reaching home and sharing their adventures with their families, they pedaled harder. As they approached Roorkee, the heat intensified, and the traffic became denser. The ride was now riskier, but the boys were more cautious. They kept a close eye on each other, making sure no one was left behind.

At one point, they encountered a pack of stray dogs that began chasing them. Laughing and shouting, the boys pedaled furiously, trying to outrun the dogs. Despite the chaos, they kept pushing forward, and soon, they saw the outskirts of Roorkee in the distance. Sweaty, tired, and covered in dust, they knew the journey was coming to an end. Yet, there was a deep sense of achievement within them. They had faced a series of hurdles—from stolen shoes to punctured tires—and had overcome them together.

Homecoming and Reflection

As they reached their neighborhood, the boys slowed down, savoring the final moments of their adventure. They stopped at Madhav's house, where the day had begun. Madhav's mother greeted them with a warm smile and a jug of cold water, which the boys drank gratefully. Sitting on the veranda, they recounted the day's events, laughing at their mishaps and celebrating their teamwork. The day had not gone as planned, but it had been made all the more memorable by the challenges they had faced together.

Madhav, who had remained calm and composed throughout the journey, looked at his friends and felt a deep sense of satisfaction. The trip to Haridwar had been more than just a visit to a holy place or a fun outing. It had been a lesson in resilience, teamwork, and friendship. Together, they had faced the heat, fatigue, punctures, and even theft, supporting each other every step of the way.

As the sun began to set, the boys realized it was time to head home. They stood up, a mix of exhaustion and contentment in their hearts. The adventure had bonded them in a way that few experiences could. As they parted ways, Madhav reflected on the day's events. It had been a difficult journey, but incredibly rewarding. He knew that no matter what challenges the future might bring, he and his friends would face them with the same courage and unity. He had seen the strength of their friendship during their visit to Haridwar, and he was certain it would carry them through anything that came their way.

"Your strength lies not in never falling, but in rising every time you do."

8

Higher Studies

Madhav always aspired to gain admission to the prestigious University of Roorkee (now IIT Roorkee) for his undergraduate engineering degree. However, fate had different plans. Despite his tireless hard work and dedication, he missed the entrance examination cut-off by just four marks. It was a heartbreaking moment, as he had dreamed of studying engineering at Roorkee. However, his close friend, Rajesh, succeeded in securing admission to an MPhil program in Instrumentation at the same university based on his MSc marks. Though disappointed, Madhav refused to let this setback define his future.

A New Opportunity: GATE

At this juncture, a new opportunity presented itself – the Graduate Aptitude Test in Engineering (GATE), which was being introduced for the first time. This exam would serve as the gateway for admission to MTech programs at the Indian Institutes of Technology (IITs). Energized by the possibilities, Madhav decided to take the exam along with three of his friends. However, since this was the inaugural GATE exam, there was very little information available about its format. None of the students had any clue how to prepare, but they approached the challenge with determination and hope.

To everyone's surprise, all four secured admission, with Madhav earning a seat at IIT Kharagpur, one of India's oldest and most prestigious IITs. This victory marked the beginning of a new chapter in Madhav's life, filled with enthusiasm and renewed ambition.

Arrival at IIT Kharagpur: A New World

Stepping into IIT Kharagpur felt like entering a world of limitless opportunities. The sprawling campus, with its iconic main building and lush greenery, was unlike anything Madhav had ever experienced before. It was not just a place for academic learning; it was a microcosm of the world itself, teeming with brilliant minds and thriving in an environment of competition, collaboration, intellectual rigor, and inspired freedom.

The first few days were a whirlwind of excitement and anticipation. As Madhav settled into his hostel, he met a diverse group of students from across India. Each new student brought with them a unique culture, language, and perspective. Conversations in the hostel rooms ranged from technical debates about engineering principles to spirited discussions about cricket and politics. This blend of diverse backgrounds and interests created an enriching atmosphere that fueled Madhav's growth both personally and academically.

The Grind: Hard Work and Preparation

Life at IIT Kharagpur was far from easy, and Madhav quickly realized the challenges ahead. The demand for the M.Tech course was high, and classes began early. Assignments piled up, and his professor, a renowned expert in his field, expected nothing short of excellence from his students. Madhav's goal wasn't merely to complete his M.Tech but to achieve excellence. He knew that securing good grades was crucial for campus recruitment, as top companies from around the world would come to hire the brightest engineers. From the start, Madhav adopted a disciplined attitude toward his studies. His days were filled with lectures, experiments in laboratories, and countless hours in the vast IIT library. The library, with its towering bookshelves and quiet reading corners, quickly became his second home.

Group Discussions and Seminars: Sharpening Minds

IIT Kharagpur placed a significant emphasis on group discussions and seminars, designed to develop communication and critical thinking skills—essential attributes for engineers in the real world. During these discussions, Madhav often found himself in the thick of heated debates. Whether it was about the intricacies of equipment or broader topics like sustainable energy, these sessions challenged him to think on his feet, defend his ideas, and appreciate the perspectives of others.

Seminars were another critical aspect of academic life. Madhav attended lectures by industry experts, professors from other IITs, and even international scholars. These seminars exposed him to cutting-edge research and emerging technologies, keeping him informed about the latest trends in the field.

The Intensity of Competition: Pushing Limits

The competition at IIT Kharagpur was intense and relentless. Many of Madhav's friends were among the brightest students in the country, and everyone was working hard to stay ahead. It wasn't just about grades; it was about standing out among a group of extraordinary talents. This fierce competition pushed Madhav to constantly improve himself. However, the competition was as healthy as it was powerful. Madhav's companions were not only competitors; they were also allies. He often collaborated on group projects with his classmates, tackling complex problems together. These projects taught him not only how to learn from others but also the importance of teamwork and collaboration.

Extracurricular Activities: Games, Music, Dance, and Dramatics

Life at IIT Kharagpur wasn't just about academics. The campus thrived with a vibrant range of extracurricular activities, and Madhav was determined to make the most of them. Sports played an integral role in campus life, with the grounds buzzing every evening as students engaged in cricket, football, and badminton. Madhav particularly enjoyed playing football with his friends, finding it to be a refreshing break from academic pressures and a great way to stay fit.

Music and dance also flourished at IIT Kharagpur, with the campus housing student clubs dedicated to various artistic forms. Madhav, who had always enjoyed music, eagerly joined the college music club. The cultural festival, one of the largest student-run events in the country, was a major highlight. It brought together talented students from all over India, featuring performances in music, dance, drama, and even stand-up comedy. For Madhav, this festival was the crowning moment of his college life, a chance to revel in the creativity and passion of his fellow students.

Dramatics: A New Challenge

Dramatics was another arena where Madhav found himself immersed. His first role in a college play was small, but the experience of being on stage and in the spotlight was exhilarating. It was a challenge entirely different from academics, giving him a chance to tap into a new, creative side of himself. Over time, Madhav grew more confident and involved in the dramatics scene, relishing the opportunities to perform and learn.

The Role of the Library: A Hub for Knowledge

The IIT Kharagpur library was more than just a place to study; it was a sanctuary for intellectual exploration. With a wealth of resources ranging from engineering textbooks to cutting-edge research papers, the library became Madhav's second home. He spent countless hours not only completing his coursework but also diving into topics beyond his curriculum. The library also facilitated study groups, where students collaborated to solve complex problems, exchange ideas, and prepare for exams, creating a rich learning environment.

Debates and Discussions: Sharpening Public Speaking Skills

In addition to group discussions, formal debates were a regular fixture at IIT Kharagpur. Organized by student clubs, these debates covered a wide spectrum of topics—from engineering ethics to the societal impact of technology. Madhav actively participated in many of these debates, refining his skills in argumentation and public speaking. The experience proved invaluable, especially when it came to job interviews, where clear and confident communication is crucial.

Campus Recruitment: The Ultimate Test

As Madhav approached the final year of his M.Tech., the pressure to perform reached its peak. Thoughts of what he would do if he didn't secure a job constantly troubled him. The campus recruitment season was just around the corner, and top companies from around the world were preparing to visit IIT Kharagpur. The competition for the best jobs was fierce, with every student vying for a position in a prestigious company. Madhav knew that his performance in the interview would be just as important as his academic record.

Determined to succeed, he started participating in mock group discussions and preparing for interviews. He attended seminars on how to excel in both technical and HR interviews, while also focusing on improving his problem-solving skills. Although the preparation was tough, Madhav was committed to putting in the effort.

Finally, the day of his first interview arrived. Despite his nervousness, he performed exceptionally well. His hard work and preparation paid off when he received an offer from a top multinational company. The sense of accomplishment was overwhelming, and he knew this was just the beginning of a bright career.

The Final Year: A Celebration of Achievements

As Madhav concluded his academic session at IIT Kharagpur, he reflected on his journey with a deep sense of pride. The late-night study sessions, intense debates, cultural festivals, and the friendships he formed along the way had all played a pivotal role in shaping him into a well-rounded individual. IIT Kharagpur had not only provided him with world-class education but also enriched his life with memories and lessons that would stay with him forever.

With his new job offer in hand, Madhav was ready to embark on the next phase of his life. IIT Kharagpur would always hold a special place in his heart—a place where he had faced challenges, celebrated victories, and discovered his true potential.

"Dreams are the whispers of your soul; listen closely, for they hold the power to guide you toward the life you were meant to live."

9

Selection in a Prestigious PSU

Madhav had always been a diligent worker with a forward-thinking mindset. So, when he was selected as Personnel Officer at ITI Limited, India's first public sector undertaking, he felt an overwhelming sense of pride and excitement. His journey began at the head office in Bengaluru, where he embarked on a rigorous training program designed to immerse him in every facet of the company, including its various departments, services, and products.

A Challenging Yet Exciting Start

The first few days in Bengaluru were both challenging and exhilarating. The corporate environment was rapidly evolving, and Madhav quickly realized that this training program was no ordinary experience. As a pioneer in his field, ITI Limited exposed him to multiple departments, each offering unique insights. He spent time in the Materials

Management (MM) department, where he learned about the complexities of supply chain management, procurement processes, and vendor negotiations.

In addition to this, Madhav had hands-on experience in the Personnel Department, where he delved into human resource management, employee relations, and workforce development. His learning wasn't confined to just personnel management. Madhav also had the opportunity to visit the Research and Development department, where engineers were pushing the boundaries of innovation, working on cutting-edge technology. The Finance department also piqued his interest, as he observed the precision with which budgets, audits, and financial forecasts were handled.

A Deep Dive into the Digital Future

The IT department left a lasting impression on Madhav. He marveled at how technology played a vital role in streamlining processes and maintaining the company's technological backbone. It was clear to him that ITI Limited was at the forefront of digital transformation, and the knowledge he gained here would prove invaluable in his career.

Brainstorming Sessions: Cultivating Creativity

One of the most dynamic aspects of Madhav's training was his participation in brainstorming sessions. ITI Limited encouraged cross-functional collaboration, and Madhav found himself in rooms full of people from diverse departments, discussing policies for improving services, generating new product ideas, and exploring ways to streamline operations. These sessions were intense, requiring creative thinking and problem-solving.

Madhav quickly learned that no idea was too small or insignificant in these discussions—every contribution mattered. The ability to think outside the box was highly valued. Initially, Madhav took a backseat, observing how others approached the discussions. But as his confidence grew, he began contributing actively. His fresh perspective, combined with his understanding of personnel management, enabled him to offer valuable ideas related to workforce optimization and employee engagement.

A Journey of Growth and Innovation

Through these brainstorming sessions, Madhav honed his critical thinking and problem-solving abilities. His experience at ITI Limited not only enhanced his professional skills but also sparked his creativity and vision for the future. What started as a rigorous training program evolved into a transformative journey, one that left a lasting impact on his career and personal growth.

Presentation Skills: A Key to Success

As part of his training at ITI Limited, Madhav was required to make presentations on various topics related to the functioning of the company. These presentations were not just about showcasing knowledge; they were a test of his communication and persuasion skills. Initially, it was intimidating to stand in front of experienced professionals and present. However, Madhav quickly adapted. He learned the importance of clarity, structure, and the use of engaging visuals. With each presentation, his confidence grew. He became skilled at tailoring his message for different audiences, whether it was a technical employee, senior management, or a potential customer.

Life Skills: Thriving in the Corporate World

The training program at ITI Limited was not just about technical knowledge; it was also about developing essential life skills that would help Madhav thrive in the demanding corporate environment. He had to juggle multiple tasks—attending training sessions, participating in meetings, preparing presentations, and completing assignments. Adaptability was a crucial life skill he quickly learned. Madhav had to adjust to varying work styles and expectations, which helped him become more versatile. Additionally, he realized the importance of networking. Building relationships with colleagues from different departments made the work environment more enjoyable and provided him with valuable insights and support.

Team Building and Collaboration

Beyond the technical training, ITI Limited placed a strong emphasis on promoting teamwork and collaboration among its employees. Madhav actively participated in various team-building activities, including corporate games and sporting events. These activities were designed to break down hierarchical barriers and foster trust among team members. Whether it was a round of table tennis, a game of cricket during lunch breaks, or moments of relaxation after work, Madhav found these experiences invaluable. They not only allowed him to connect with his colleagues but also taught him essential lessons in teamwork, leadership, and communication. Working together outside of the office led to better collaboration in the workplace, strengthening the overall work culture.

Boardroom Meetings: The Art of Communication and Decision-Making

One of the most challenging aspects of Madhav's training was attending boardroom meetings. These meetings were held in a high-risk environment with top-level management, where crucial decisions were made. Senior executives reviewed performance metrics, made important business decisions, and discussed strategies. As a trainee, Madhav initially felt intimidated by the seriousness of these meetings. However, he soon realized that they were a great learning opportunity.

Madhav observed that communication was key in these meetings. Each participant had to briefly present their ideas and support them with data. He watched how senior officials expressed their views, asked insightful questions, and made decisions under pressure. Madhav learned that effective communication is not just about speaking well—it's also about listening carefully, analyzing information quickly, and making the right decisions at the right time.

Listening Skills: A Critical Competence

Throughout his training, Madhav realized that listening is one of the most underestimated but essential skills in the corporate world. Whether in meetings, brainstorming sessions, or informal conversations with colleagues, careful listening allowed him to gather valuable information.

Effective listening also helped Madhav build stronger relationships with his coworkers. By listening attentively and understanding others' viewpoints, he gained their trust and respect. This skill became especially vital when he moved to the personnel department, where handling employee concerns and mediating conflicts required a deep understanding of people's emotions and motivations.

Stress Management: Balancing Work and Well-being

The demands of Madhav's training program were immense, and at times, the pressure felt overwhelming. Presentations, boardroom meetings, deadlines, and the constant need to perform took a toll on his mental and physical health. However, ITI Limited recognized the importance of stress management. As part of his life skills training, Madhav attended several stress management workshops.

These workshops introduced techniques such as mindfulness, deep breathing exercises, and time-out strategies to help manage stress. Madhav learned the significance of maintaining a healthy work-life balance—regular exercise, a proper sleep schedule, and taking breaks during work became essential parts of his daily routine.

Madhav also discovered that speaking with his superiors and colleagues about the challenges he faced was an effective way to relieve stress. The company fostered a culture of open communication, which provided a supportive environment to manage the pressures of the corporate world.

Transfer to the Naini Unit, Allahabad

After successfully completing his training in Bengaluru, Madhav was transferred to the Naini Unit in Allahabad (now Prayagraj). ITI Limited, one of the major manufacturing plants in the region, was a key part of the Naini Unit. This move introduced a whole new set of challenges. While his training in Bengaluru had been more theoretical, focusing on learning about different departments, his role in Naini was far more practical.

At Naini, Madhav was expected to apply the skills he had learned during his training—whether it was improving operational efficiency, managing personnel, or handling employee complaints. The hands-on experience he gained in the new unit helped him develop a deeper understanding of the challenges involved in running a manufacturing plant. His training in Bengaluru had equipped him with knowledge, but it was at Naini where he truly honed his skills.

Growth and Challenges in Naini

In Naini, Madhav's role was no longer about learning but about implementation. He was expected to take charge and apply the knowledge he had gained. Whether it was improving processes or resolving conflicts, the stakes were higher, and the pressure was greater. But the experience was invaluable. His time spent in presentations, brainstorming sessions, and boardroom meetings in Bengaluru proved to be immensely helpful in tackling the real-world issues he faced at Naini.

Madhav's communication and leadership skills were put to the test. He had to collaborate with teams across different departments, ensure smooth operations, and address concerns raised by employees. Every challenge was an opportunity to grow, and Madhav embraced them with determination and a problem-solving mindset.

Conclusion: A Journey of Growth and Success

Madhav's journey from an intern to a personnel officer at the Naini Unit marked a significant phase of growth and self-discovery. The skills he developed during his training in Bengaluru, combined with the hands-on experience at Naini, helped him master crucial life skills. These included communication, active listening, and stress management—essential tools for thriving in the corporate world.

As Madhav progressed in his career at ITI Limited, he realized that the lessons he had learned during his training were not just useful in his professional life but were also instrumental in his personal growth. With newfound confidence in his abilities, Madhav was prepared to face the challenges ahead, knowing that each experience would help shape him into a better leader.

"Your career is not just a path you follow; it's the legacy you build with passion, perseverance, and the courage to pursue your true purpose."

10

Madhav's Journey at ITI Naini: Embracing New Challenges and Building a Strong Team

Madhav was overjoyed when he received the appointment letter for a position in the Human Resources Department at ITI Naini, a prestigious industrial unit located in Allahabad (now Prayagraj). It felt like a dream come true. His parents had always hoped that if he were transferred to Prayagraj, he would get the opportunity to bathe in the Sangam every day. After being selected through campus placements, Madhav felt a mix of pride and nervousness as he prepared to begin his professional career in the manpower section. Little did he know that his early days at the company would present him with unexpected challenges.

First Day Jitters and Unexpected Questions

Madhav's first day at ITI Naini was filled with excitement and a touch of anxiety. As he walked into the Human Resources department, he was greeted by a mixture of welcoming faces and curious gazes. However, instead of a formal welcome, some senior officers immediately began questioning him.

"How did you get this job?" one officer asked, his tone making Madhav uncomfortable. "Who recommended your name?" another officer inquired, doubt evident in his voice. The most shocking question came when someone casually asked, "How much did you pay for this position?"

Madhav was stunned. He had never anticipated such questions, especially on his first day. The unexpected interrogation made him feel insulted, and his nervousness only deepened. For a moment, he didn't know how to respond. After calming himself, he answered confidently, "I was selected through campus recruitment." The officers maintained eye contact but didn't press the matter further. This unsettling experience made Madhav question his decisions. He wondered if his job at ITI Naini would be more challenging than he had expected. He realized that to succeed, he would need to quickly adapt to the new environment.

Navigating a New Work Environment and Culture

Madhav spent time with his seniors and fellow officers to understand the work culture at ITI Naini. The manpower section, where he began working, was responsible for managing the unit's staffing needs, recruitment, and selection processes. The work atmosphere was a blend of rigid hierarchy and camaraderie among the lower-level workers.

As he observed, Madhav noticed a pervasive sense of distrust between the management and the workers, which was exacerbated by the strong influence of labor unions. ITI Naini had a rich history of labor union activities. The unions frequently held meetings, demanding better working conditions and sometimes organizing protests. This was a new experience for Madhav, who had studied labor relations in his human resources course, but witnessing it firsthand was an entirely different challenge.

The unions played a significant role in decision-making processes, and Madhav had to learn how to navigate through this complex network. It became clear to him that building strong relationships, understanding the dynamics of the workplace, and managing the delicate balance between the management and workers would be crucial to his success.

A Journey of Growth and Adaptation

Madhav's early days at ITI Naini were full of learning and unexpected hurdles. But with each passing day, he gained valuable insights into human resources management in a real-world setting. The challenges he faced—whether from unexpected questions or navigating union relations—helped him build resilience. Slowly but surely, he began adapting to his new role, knowing that his journey at ITI Naini would be one of growth, teamwork, and overcoming obstacles.

Building Friendships and Forming a Strong Team

Despite facing initial challenges, Madhav found unwavering support from his colleagues. Within a few months, he had established a close-knit group of coworkers who shared lunch together every day.

Lunchtime discussions shifted from casual topics to work-related matters, transforming these moments into opportunities for team building and bonding. Each team member brought their own lunch, allowing everyone to enjoy a variety of dishes. During these lunch sessions, conversations often delved into the various functions of their unit. Madhav's friends, some of whom had been working at ITI Naini for years, generously shared their experiences—from handling labor unions to managing employee grievances. These discussions provided Madhav with invaluable insights into the inner workings of the unit. He learned about the intricacies of labor laws, the importance of listening to employee concerns, and how to effectively balance the demands of both management and labor unions. What started as casual camaraderie soon turned into mentorship, helping Madhav navigate the unique culture of ITI Naini.

Labor Union Activities and Effective Problem-Solving

One of the most significant challenges Madhav faced was the labor union's involvement in every major decision. While unions played a vital role in protecting workers' rights, their presence sometimes complicated the decision-making process. Grievances often escalated into union matters, which made it difficult to resolve them swiftly.

One particular situation stood out: Madhav was tasked with addressing a grievance regarding the unfair allocation of overtime shifts. Union representatives argued that some workers were being overburdened, while others were excluded, creating unrest among employees. Rather than following the usual top-down approach, where management issues directives, Madhav decided to take a more collaborative approach. He gathered feedback from both workers and their supervisors, carefully listening to their concerns. Madhav then arranged a meeting with union leaders and presented a solution that involved distributing overtime shifts more fairly, ensuring equal opportunities for all workers to earn additional pay.

This approach not only resolved the immediate issue but also helped Madhav build trust with the union members. By valuing their input and involving them in the decision-making process, he earned their respect. It was a small victory, but it greatly boosted Madhav's confidence in his ability to handle complex workplace issues and find solutions that worked for everyone involved.

Listening and Teamwork: Keys to Success

Over time, Madhav realized that one of the most important skills for his role was the ability to listen. Whether it was an employee's individual complaint or a labor union's collective demand, being an attentive listener allowed him to identify the root cause of problems and work toward effective solutions. Madhav also understood the immense value of teamwork. The relationships he built during lunch breaks played a crucial role in his success. Whenever he faced a challenge, whether it was drafting a new policy or resolving a dispute, his friends and colleagues were there to support him. Together, they solved problems, shared ideas, and found creative solutions. Madhav's team became his backbone, and the camaraderie they shared made even the toughest days bearable. His fresh perspective and knowledge from his recent education made him a valuable team member.

Building a Strong Team and Securing a Bright Future

By the end of his third month at ITI Naini, Madhav had overcome the initial hurdles and transformed into a confident, capable professional. His ability to adapt to new environments, solve complex problems, and work collaboratively earned him respect not only within the HR department but also beyond. His exposure to various functions, from labor relations to policy development, broadened his understanding of the complexities involved in managing an industrial workforce.

Thanks to the strong team he had built, Madhav was able to navigate the challenging terrain of trade union activities and employee grievances with ease. His journey at ITI Naini had only just begun, but the foundation he laid during his first three months set the stage for a successful future. Madhav had learned that success in such a dynamic environment required empathy, teamwork, and the ability to listen and adapt—not just technical knowledge. With a strong team and honed skills, Madhav was confident in his ability to tackle any challenge the ever-evolving world of HR might present.

"***Every small step forward, no matter how slow, brings you closer to the greatness you are destined to achieve.***"

11

Madhav's First Challenge: Reforming the Transport Services

Stepping into a Strategic Role

Madhav was renowned for his strategic mind and commitment to efficiency. When entrusted with managing the Transport Services Department in the Naini Unit of ITI Limited, he knew he was stepping into a crucial but challenging role. Though not glamorous, the department's work was vital to the smooth functioning of the company.

The responsibility was immense: managing a fleet of over 52 private buses tasked with transporting employees from urban and rural areas to the workplace. This service was the lifeline connecting employees in remote locations to the company.

A System Plagued by Corruption

However, Madhav quickly realized that the transport system was riddled with inefficiencies and corruption. Over time, transporters had manipulated bus routes for their personal gain. Bribes flowed freely, and brokers ensured certain buses continued operating despite their inefficiency.

The result? Unnecessary detours inflated fuel costs, buses ran half-empty, and the system had become unsustainable. Employees endured longer commutes while the company's expenses skyrocketed. Madhav understood that these issues could no longer be ignored if the company aimed to control operating costs and improve productivity.

The First Steps Towards Reform

Taking over the department, Madhav initially felt overwhelmed by the extent of the problem. Costs were spiraling, and previous efforts to rationalize the system had been minimal. Determined to bring change, he embarked on a meticulous review of the transport system.

For days, Madhav analyzed the data:

- Routes covered by each bus.
- Occupancy rates.
- Geographical distribution of employees.

What he uncovered was shocking. Some buses made unnecessarily long detours to accommodate favored stops, while others operated nearly empty. Employees living in close proximity were scattered across multiple buses, even when fewer vehicles could have sufficed. It became evident that deliberate sabotage had infiltrated the system, benefiting a select few at the company's expense.

Crafting a Plan for Efficiency

Madhav knew that transforming the transport system would require bold decisions and thorough planning. Armed with data, he devised a comprehensive plan to rationalize routes and reduce the fleet size while ensuring employee convenience. His goals were clear:

- **Cut Costs:** Eliminate inefficiencies to significantly lower expenditure.
- **Enhance Utilization:** Optimize bus occupancy by reorganizing routes.
- **Maintain Comfort:** Ensure employees could travel to and from work with ease.

The Road Ahead

Madhav's journey was bound to be met with resistance. Overcoming entrenched corruption and vested interests would not be easy. Yet, his unwavering determination to create a transparent and efficient system set the foundation for the reforms to come.

With data-driven strategies and a clear vision, Madhav was ready to face the challenges ahead and prove that efficiency and integrity could transform even the most deeply flawed systems.

Resistance to Change

As expected, resistance came swiftly. The agents, whose livelihoods depended on keeping their buses on the road, were furious. They saw Madhav's efforts as a threat to their easy arrangements. Many of these agents had secured their contracts through under-the-table deals, and they were determined to protect their interests.

The backlash was intense. Madhav faced a barrage of complaints, both informal and formal. Some agents went so far as to lodge official grievances against him, aiming to tarnish his reputation and halt his review of the routes. Transporters, fearing disruption to their profits, even attempted to sow discord within the department.

Unyielding Determination

Despite the mounting pressure, Madhav remained steadfast. He was confident that management would back him if he presented a strong, data-driven proposal. His vision was crystal clear: to create a transportation system that was both cost-effective and reliable.

Madhav knew that success required the support of his colleagues, especially those with years of experience and a deep understanding of the department's workings.

Winning Over the Team

To gain their trust, Madhav organized a series of meetings with his team. During these sessions, he presented his findings, highlighting how the current system was hemorrhaging money due to inefficiencies.

At first, skepticism lingered. However, Madhav's unwavering determination began to inspire his colleagues. They saw that he wasn't simply trying to cut costs for the sake of it—he had a well-thought-out plan that prioritized long-term benefits for both the company and its employees. Gradually, the team began to rally behind him.

Rationalizing Routes

With his team's support, Madhav embarked on a major overhaul of the transportation system. He re-mapped routes, consolidated operations, and reduced the number of buses in service without compromising quality. Employees from nearby areas were grouped together, minimizing redundancy.

For those in remote or rural locations, Madhav ensured that their transportation needs were still met with timely and efficient routes. This meticulous planning ensured no one was left behind.

Presenting the Vision

Within just 15 days, Madhav prepared a comprehensive report for the management. The report detailed the proposed changes, including new routes, projected cost savings, and enhanced coordination mechanisms.

Madhav's plan wasn't just about slashing expenses—it was about creating a sustainable system capable of adapting to future shifts in employee distribution. According to his estimates, the company could reduce transportation costs by an impressive 40%.

A Blueprint for the Future

Madhav's report also included measures to improve communication between bus operators and staff, ensuring that any changes would be implemented smoothly. His focus wasn't merely on efficiency but on fostering a system that could grow with the company's needs.

Through determination, collaboration, and a clear vision, Madhav transformed resistance into opportunity, setting a new standard for cost-effective and reliable employee transportation.

Madhav's Plan: A New Era for Transportation

The management was thoroughly impressed with Madhav's proposal. His plan was not only data-driven but also practical and well-thought-out. It didn't take long for the management to approve his proposal, giving him the green light to implement the changes.

The Agents' Resistance

However, the agents were angry. Their complaints had been falling on deaf ears up until this point. But Madhav had successfully proven that the old system was inefficient, and the potential savings from his new plan were undeniable.

Transformation in Action

Once Madhav's new transportation system was implemented, the results were evident almost immediately. The number of buses on the road was reduced, and the remaining fleet was optimized for better efficiency. Employees noticed a positive change in their commutes, with many appreciating the improvements that made their journeys more streamlined.

Building a Strong Team

Madhav didn't stop at just the plan; he also assembled a team that shared his vision of fairness and efficiency. Together, they worked to ensure the smooth implementation and long-term success of the system.

A Benchmark for Change

Madhav's journey became a benchmark within ITI Limited. His story proved that with clear vision, determination, and proper planning, lasting change can be achieved—even in the face of resistance.

"True change begins with a clear vision and unwavering determination. With the right team and a plan for progress, even the toughest challenges can be transformed into lasting success."

12

Title: The Journey of Confidence – Madhav's Transformation at the HRD Centre

The First Day: Anxiety and Anticipation

Madhav's first day at the Human Resource Development (HRD) Center was filled with a mix of excitement and anxiety. As an officer responsible for conducting and developing training programs, his role demanded frequent public speaking and interaction—something Madhav had never been comfortable with. He always felt a sense of dread at the thought of standing before a room full of trainees. Employees expected guidance from someone confident and knowledgeable, but Madhav questioned if he could live up to their expectations.

The HRD Center was buzzing with activity. The training department's responsibility was vast: ensuring employees, from entry-level workers to senior management, were up-to-date with the latest industry standards, technologies, and management practices. It was also in charge of training under the Apprenticeship Act, ensuring all trainees received the required training by law.

Facing the Challenge: The First Training Hall Visit

When Madhav stepped into the training hall for the first time, his throat tightened, and his hands trembled slightly. The thought of addressing a room full of trainees and staff filled him with anxiety. Would he be able to handle the responsibility? Would his lack of experience in public speaking lead to failure? These were the thoughts that clouded his mind.

However, Madhav wasn't alone in this journey. Mr. Sharma, the experienced in-charge of the training department, noticed his nervousness and extended a reassuring hand. He shared that the fear Madhav felt was not unfamiliar. "I too had such fears when I started," Mr. Sharma said, offering Madhav guidance and support throughout this journey.

Understanding the Training Process: Breaking It Down

Madhav continued to train under Mr. Sharma's mentorship for several days, gradually becoming familiar with the workings of the training department. Mr. Sharma broke down the entire training process into manageable steps: creating a training calendar, assessing training needs, planning brainstorming sessions, and handling feedback.

Training needs assessment was the cornerstone of any successful program. It involved evaluating employees' existing skill sets, identifying gaps, and determining the training required to bridge those gaps. Madhav quickly learned that this was no simple task. It required careful coordination with department heads and valuable feedback from employees. Mr. Sharma explained that they would review performance reports, conduct interviews, and sometimes even run surveys to understand what training was necessary.

Stepping Up: Gaining Confidence

Once the team had a clear understanding of the training needs, they moved on to the planning phase. Madhav assisted in gathering data from across the organization, collecting feedback, talking to supervisors, and identifying areas where employees felt they needed more training. At first, each conversation felt stressful, but as time passed, Madhav's confidence grew. The more he engaged with employees, the more he realized that his role wasn't just about speaking in front of people—it was about facilitating their growth and development.

Madhav's hesitations began to melt away as he recognized the impact he could have. He wasn't just a trainer; he was a mentor, a guide, and a facilitator of positive change.

Conclusion: Embracing Growth and Building Confidence

With each passing day, Madhav's transformation became evident. What began as a daunting challenge had evolved into an opportunity for growth, not only for the employees but for himself as well. His journey at the HRD Center was not just about public speaking; it was about developing the confidence to lead, empower, and shape the future of the workforce.

Through patience, practice, and guidance from Mr. Sharma, Madhav not only overcame his fear of public speaking but also discovered his true potential as a leader in the HRD field.

Creating the Training Calendar

Once the training needs had been assessed, the next step was to prepare a comprehensive training calendar for the year. This included scheduling sessions on technical skills, soft skills, leadership, compliance, and the rules and regulations under the Apprenticeship Act. The goal was to strike a balance—ensuring that the training programs did not disrupt regular work, while also providing ample learning opportunities.

Collaborating with Department Heads

Madhav, under the guidance of Mr. Sharma, organized a meeting with various department heads to finalize the training calendar. However, he struggled to assert his ideas during these meetings. The other managers were far more experienced, and Madhav often found himself feeling intimidated. Despite this, Mr. Sharma encouraged everyone to speak up and contribute their suggestions.

A New Perspective

During one of the meetings, Madhav proposed an idea he felt strongly about: a well-rounded mix of training sessions. He suggested that the calendar should include technical sessions, leadership development, industrial relations training, and problem-solving workshops. Additionally, he recommended spacing the sessions evenly to avoid overwhelming the teams.

To his surprise, Madhav's idea was well received. The manager agreed with his suggestions, and it was decided to incorporate a balance of different sessions throughout the year. Madhav actively contributed to shaping the calendar, suggesting team-building workshops and time management training.

Growing Confidence and Involvement

As the process continued, Madhav began to feel more confident. What started as a feeling of being a novice gradually transformed into a sense of belonging. He no longer felt out of place in these meetings and became an integral part of the team. His involvement grew, and he was trusted to organize and conduct the training programs.

Through this experience, Madhav not only played a key role in planning the training calendar but also gained valuable skills in leadership, collaboration, and communication, marking his growth into an essential member of the team.

Conducting the First Training Program

The real challenge for Madhav was public speaking. Although he had become proficient in planning and evaluating, he had never conducted a training session on his own. Recognizing this, Mr. Sharma suggested that Madhav co-lead a session on the Apprenticeship Act. He advised Madhav to think of the session as a conversation. "You've done the research, you know the material—now it's just about presenting it," he said.

The day of the training arrived. Standing in front of the audience, Madhav's heart raced. He glanced at Mr. Sharma, who gave him an encouraging nod. Madhav took a deep breath and began speaking. The first few minutes were shaky, but as the session progressed, something changed. The more he spoke, the more comfortable he became. Employees responded well, asking questions and participating in discussions. By the end of the session, Madhav felt a surge of accomplishment. The positive feedback was overwhelming. One participant described the session as "clear, concise, and informative." Madhav had explained the Apprenticeship Act in a way that made it easy for everyone to understand. These encouraging comments boosted his confidence and assured him that he was on the right path.

Mastering the Art of Brainstorming

With his first training session under his belt, Madhav's responsibilities began to grow. He was soon tasked with facilitating brainstorming sessions, a crucial part of training programs. These sessions allowed employees to share ideas, solve problems collaboratively, and innovate in their roles. At first, leading the brainstorming sessions seemed challenging. How could he encourage people to speak and share their ideas?

Once again, Mr. Sharma stepped in with advice. "Your job is to guide the conversation, not dominate it," he explained. "Ask open-ended questions, listen carefully, and make sure everyone feels heard."

During his first brainstorming session, Madhav put this advice into practice. He asked insightful questions, and gradually, employees began to open up. Ideas flowed freely, and by the end of the session, several practical solutions had been proposed. Madhav realized that team-building was happening naturally. Employees who once worked in silos were now collaborating, sharing ideas, and supporting each other. Madhav understood that his role wasn't just about training; it was about fostering an environment of collaboration and innovation.

Negotiation and Bargaining

Madhav's responsibilities had grown, demanding that he refine his skills in persuasion, negotiation, and bargaining. Department heads often requested more training sessions than the calendar could accommodate. At other times, budgets were tight, requiring compromises.

Madhav mastered the art of negotiation by carefully balancing the needs of the departments with the limitations of the organization. He worked closely with managers to prioritize the most essential training programs, ensuring that crucial skills were never overlooked. His effective negotiation skills earned him the respect of his colleagues.

The Final Transformation

A remarkable transformation had taken place in Madhav. He had gone from a hesitant individual to a confident training officer. Madhav could now lead sessions, facilitate brainstorming, and interact with senior managers with ease. Training feedback consistently praised his clarity, approachability, and his ability to engage participants.

Mr. Sharma's final response to Madhav was simple yet profound: "You have made great progress," he said. "Training is not just about teaching others; it's about constantly learning yourself." Madhav smiled, feeling a deep sense of accomplishment. He had not only overcome his fears but had also helped countless employees advance in their careers. As he looked at the new training calendar filled with workshops and sessions he had designed for the upcoming year, he knew his development journey had only just begun.

Conclusion

Madhav's story is one of both personal and professional growth. What started as a fear of public speaking evolved into one of his greatest strengths as he gained experience and confidence. With the unwavering support of his mentor, Mr. Sharma, and his dedication to learning the complexities of training needs assessment, scheduling, and facilitation, Madhav overcame his initial hesitation and became an effective training officer.

His journey illustrates the power of persistence, the importance of teamwork, and the skill of negotiation and persuasion in a professional setting. The lessons Madhav learned shaped his approach to training and development, ensuring that both he and his trainees were always striving for continuous improvement.

"True growth begins when you face your fears, embrace learning, and transform challenges into stepping stones. Your journey of self-improvement is the key to unlocking not only your potential but the potential of those you lead."

13

A Memorable Journey to Rajpur – Madhav's Wedding Adventure in 1986

Madhav, a resident of Allahabad (now Prayagraj), originally from Bihar, was preparing for an exciting yet nerve-wracking event - his wedding. The marriage had been arranged with a prosperous family in Rajpur village, located in Rohtas district of Bihar. Madhav was filled with excitement but also anxiety. He wondered how the wedding procession would travel from Allahabad to Rajpur, how many guests would attend, and what preparations would need to be made for them. His mind was entangled in these thoughts, making him restless.

The Big Day: The Journey Begins

The day arrived when the wedding procession was set to leave for Rajpur. It was May of 1986, and the atmosphere was buzzing with anticipation. Madhav's friends, many of whom had never attended a traditional Bihari wedding, were eager to experience the customs and festivities.

At around 10 pm, the wedding procession of 50 people, including five women, boarded a bus bound for Rajpur. The bus ride was filled with lively chatter, laughter, and excitement as the group anticipated the adventure that awaited them. The friends from Allahabad had no idea what lay ahead, but they were sure that they were about to witness something unforgettable.

Arrival at Rajpur Village: Welcoming the Guests

The journey to Rajpur was long, and the group spent the night traveling while having fun and creating memories. They finally reached Rajpur early the next morning. The fresh air and natural beauty of the village welcomed them, setting the perfect tone for the occasion. Madhav's in-laws had made excellent arrangements for the wedding procession's stay and meals.

Temporary housing had been set up near their house, ensuring that the guests were comfortable. The hosts greeted them warmly, and a delicious traditional Bihari breakfast was served, showcasing the hospitality that the region is famous for. As the day progressed, the village began to buzz with the sounds of wedding preparations. The celebration was scheduled for the evening, and a grand pandal (canopy) was set up in a nearby field.

A Day of Rest and Anticipation

With the evening celebration still hours away, the guests from Allahabad took the opportunity to relax and soak in the village's charm. They spent the day admiring the scenery, chatting, and preparing for the evening's grand event. The anticipation of the wedding rituals only heightened the excitement.

Evening Rituals: Tilak and Matri Puja

As the sun began to set, the evening's festivities kicked off with the Tilak ceremony at 7 pm. This ritual marked the official welcome of the groom and his party into the bride's family. Madhav was adorned with flower garlands, gifts, and blessings as the bride's family honored him in a ceremony full of color and joy. This ceremony symbolized the groom's acceptance into the bride's family and was a vital part of the wedding celebrations.

Madhav's friends, who had never witnessed such traditions before, were captivated by the colorful decorations and rich cultural customs.

The Tilak ceremony was followed by the **Matri Puja**, a sacred ritual performed by the groom's family. In this puja, the blessings of the Mother Goddess were sought for the well-being and prosperous married life of the bride and groom. The air was filled with the sound of chants, mantras, and the ringing of bells as the religious rituals continued late into the evening, adding a divine aura to the celebrations.

Entertainment in the Pandal and the Villagers' Involvement

After the religious rituals, the focus shifted to entertainment, and the hosts had arranged for local artists to showcase traditional music and dance, captivating the guests. For Madhav's friends, this unexpected gift added a special charm to the evening. The atmosphere was charged with cultural vibrancy, and the rustic charm of the village made everything even more enchanting.

Madhav's friends from Allahabad, who were accustomed to different social norms and more urban settings, eagerly embraced the festivities. They wanted to dance and enjoy the evening freely, but the villagers, with their strong adherence to tradition, had other expectations. Some elders in the village felt that the guests from Allahabad should follow the customs and show respect to the traditions of the place. This created a subtle tension that lingered throughout the evening.

Among the guests was Madhav's closest friend, a Muslim from Allahabad. In rural Bihar, caste and religious divisions were still deeply entrenched at the time. Although Madhav had no objections to including his Muslim friend in the wedding celebrations, the villagers were initially uncomfortable with the idea of a Muslim participating in a traditional Brahmin marriage. In a conservative village where caste dynamics were still rigid, this sparked unease.

Sensing the tension, the groom's family cleverly introduced Madhav’s Muslim friend under a different name, presenting him as one of the groom's uncles. This subtle change in identity helped ease any potential conflict and allowed everyone to enjoy the festivities without further complications. Despite the cultural and religious differences, the evening continued without incident, and Madhav's Muslim friend joined in the joyous occasion with no further challenges.

Pari Chhavan, Kangana Bandhan, and Kanya Dan: The Rituals of Unity

As the night grew deeper, the focus shifted to the more intimate and personal rituals of the wedding. The Pariparcha ceremony, where the groom is dressed and adorned by his close relatives, began in full swing. Madhav, with a shy smile on his face, sat as his family members vied for the honor of ensuring he looked his best for the big moment.

This was followed by the Kangan Bandhan ceremony, in which a sacred thread, called a bangle, was tied on the wrists of both the bride and the groom. This thread symbolized protection and was believed to ward off any evil spirits during the wedding. As the elders blessed the couple and wished them a prosperous and harmonious union, the atmosphere became deeply emotional. The community's blessings filled the air, marking the sacred union of the couple with love, faith, and tradition.

The Sacred Moment: Kanya Daan

The defining moment of the night arrived with the Kanya Daan, one of the most revered rituals in Hindu weddings. It is a formal gift, given by the bride's father to the groom, symbolizing the bride's transition from her father's care to her new life with her husband. Madhav's bride, resplendent in a red saree and adorned with intricate gold jewellery, was brought to the mandap (wedding altar). The bride's father gently placed her hand in Madhav's, marking a profound moment of emotional significance.

Celebrating Love and New Beginnings: Swagat Aarti, Moh Dikhai, and Chauthari

After the wedding rituals were completed, the bride was ready to formally enter her new home. While the actual journey to Allahabad would take place later, the symbolic gesture of welcoming the bride into her new life was performed with the Swagat Aarti. In this Hindu ritual of worship, the bride was welcomed by her new family with a traditional Aarti.

The next morning, the final few rituals took place, including the Moh Dikhai ceremony, where the bride's face was revealed to the groom's family. This tradition symbolizes the acceptance and blessings for the new bride as she embarks on her journey with her new family.

The day culminated with the Chauthari ritual, where the couple and their families offered prayers at a small outdoor shrine. They made offerings to the family deities, seeking blessings for the newlyweds and their shared future.

A Journey of Togetherness: The Return to Allahabad

After the wedding celebrations concluded, the wedding procession began preparing for the return journey to Allahabad. However, a small dispute arose among the group. Madhav's friends, particularly those not bound by traditional Brahmin dietary restrictions, requested non-vegetarian food for the trip. Some members of the group objected, feeling it was inappropriate to consume non-vegetarian food so soon after such a sacred event. Despite the differing opinions, a compromise was reached, and arrangements were made to satisfy everyone's preferences.

The bus journey back to Allahabad was filled with light-hearted jokes, stories, and reflections on the unforgettable experience in Rajpur village. For Madhav, his wedding day was not only the beginning of a new life with his bride but also a testament to how love, friendship, and respect for each other's beliefs could transcend cultural and religious boundaries.

Madhav's friends returned home with cherished memories of a traditional Bihari wedding, and the bonds of friendship grew even stronger, forged through this shared, meaningful adventure.

"True love and respect bridge all boundaries, and it is through the union of hearts, traditions, and understanding that we embark on the most beautiful journeys of life."

14

A Journey of Faith and Fear – Madhav's Experience at the Maha Kumbh Mela (1989)

Introduction: The Call of the Maha Kumbh Mela

In 1989, the anticipation surrounding the Maha Kumbh Mela, one of the world's largest religious gatherings, reached its peak. Held every 12 years on the sacred banks of the Ganges in Allahabad (now Prayagraj), this monumental event attracts millions of Hindu devotees. The Kumbh Mela is a pilgrimage to the Triveni Sangam, where the Ganges, Yamuna, and the legendary Saraswati rivers meet. Madhav, a man of unwavering faith and insatiable curiosity, had long been captivated by the stories of its grandeur. The religious significance, the sea of sadhus, gurus, and the throngs of devotees fascinated him. This year, Madhav made the momentous decision to attend the Maha Kumbh Mela for the first time, accompanied by eight relatives. Little did they know that this sacred journey would be filled not only with devotion and joy but also with moments of fear and uncertainty.

Arrival at the Maha Kumbh Mela

As Madhav and his group of relatives arrived at the Maha Kumbh Mela, they were immediately overwhelmed by the vastness of the site. The ground stretched for miles, covered in a sprawling tented settlement. Makeshift huts, civic facilities, and impromptu markets dotted the area. The state government had set up a temporary township to accommodate the millions of pilgrims from across India and beyond. The atmosphere was a unique blend of devotion and vibrant energy. Everywhere Madhav looked, there was a crowd—some chanting, some praying, while many were preparing for the sacred bath in the holy Ganges.

The sight of thousands of pilgrims walking toward the river was unforgettable. Sadhus, gurus, and preachers sat under large pandals (tents) and delivered inspiring sermons and bhajans (devotional songs). The air reverberated with the sound of bhajans, infusing the atmosphere with a divine sense of bliss. Groups of devotees sat together, reverently listening to the words of wisdom shared by their revered saints.

The Spiritual Presence of the Sadhus

Among the most fascinating aspects of the Kumbh Mela was the presence of the sadhus—men who had renounced the material world to dedicate themselves to spiritual pursuits. Many of these sadhus had journeyed from remote corners of the Himalayas. Dressed in saffron robes or even covered in ashes, they symbolized their detachment from worldly desires. Some sadhus were deep in meditation, while others wandered through the crowds, blessing those who sought their guidance.

Madhav and his group found themselves at a pandal where a famous guru was delivering a sermon on the significance of karma, life, and death. The guru's words resonated deeply with Madhav. Despite being a devout believer, he had never before experienced spirituality on such an awe-inspiring scale. The guru's voice echoed through the pandal, drawing hundreds of devotees closer. He spoke of the sacred bath in the river and how it not only purifies the body but also the soul, freeing one from the cycle of rebirth.

Immersed in Spirituality

Madhav and his group spent the next few days exploring the vast Kumbh Mela grounds, each step immersed in the spiritual energy that surrounded them. They visited various Akharas, where different sects of sadhus gathered to share their philosophies. The atmosphere was one of deep devotion. Even the most weary travelers felt rejuvenated in this ocean of spirituality, as the divine presence seemed to infuse them with energy and peace.

Madhav's experience at the Maha Kumbh Mela became more than just a pilgrimage; it was a journey that touched both his heart and soul. Surrounded by millions of fellow devotees, he realized that this holy gathering was not only about physical purification but also about spiritual renewal. The fair was a reminder of the eternal bond that connects all believers, regardless of their backgrounds, to the divine.

The Holy Dip in the Ganga

The main event for Madhav and his relatives was the sacred bath in the Ganga. According to Hindu belief, bathing in the Ganges during the Kumbh Mela washes away all sins and grants spiritual knowledge. This moment was the one they had all been eagerly waiting for.

The excitement was palpable as they headed toward the riverbank. The crowd was growing denser near the ghat. The Ganga glistened in the morning sunlight, and its waters shimmered with divine purity. The ghats were packed with devotees. Some people had already dipped into the water, while others patiently waited for their turn. Mantras filled the air as devotees took their dips, their faces glowing with reverence and joy.

Madhav walked toward the water, holding hands with his family. The cool touch of the river sent a shiver down his spine—it was a feeling of renewal. One by one, everyone took a dip, prayed, and sought blessings from Ganga Mai. As they finished their holy bath, Madhav looked around, feeling a deep sense of contentment and peace. A dip in the Ganges was more than just a religious act; it was a profound moment of connection with something greater than themselves.

Panic in the Crowd

As they were preparing to leave the pier, disaster struck. The crowd had turned chaotic. In the midst of it, Madhav's 12-year-old nephew, Raghav, got separated from the group and disappeared into the sea of people. Panic spread instantly, and the family began calling his name. But the noise of the crowd drowned out their voices, and there was no response.

Madhav's heart raced as they frantically searched for Raghav. They pushed through the crowd, but there was no sign of him. With every passing minute, the feeling of helplessness grew stronger. In today's world, with cell phones and modern communication, finding someone lost in such a crowd would be easier. But in 1989, the only way to locate a lost person was through the public address stations scattered throughout the fair.

Madhav and his family rushed to the nearest announcement center. There, they found a large group of people anxiously waiting for news of their missing loved ones. The line was long, and the chances of finding Raghav seemed slim. Madhav's legs grew weak, and his mind was overwhelmed with fear. Thoughts of what could have happened to the young boy in such a massive crowd flooded his mind.

Hours of Anxiety

The hours that followed were the longest of Madhav's life. He and his relatives split up to search different areas of the fair, asking everyone they encountered if they had seen a boy matching Raghav's description. But every answer was negative. The announcement center kept calling out the names of the missing, but Raghav's name was never mentioned. Physically and mentally exhausted, Madhav found himself on the verge of despair. The festive air that once filled the fair now felt suffocating, and the spiritual energy that had once been uplifting now seemed disorganized and heavy. As the evening wore on, the group's hopes began to fade.

A Miracle in the Chaos

Ten long hours had passed since Raghav went missing. The fear of something untoward happening was now creeping in when suddenly, a harsh voice echoed through the loudspeaker: "We have found a child named Raghav, approximately twelve years old. His family is requested to come to the Lost and Found Center."

Madhav's heart leapt with joy, unsure if he had heard right. He rushed toward the center, his heart pounding. When he arrived, he saw Raghav standing there, looking tired but safe. Overwhelmed with relief and gratitude, Madhav's eyes filled with tears as he hugged the boy tightly.

Raghav explained that, in the confusion, he had wandered off in the wrong direction and soon found himself lost in the crowd. After hours of aimless wandering, a volunteer finally spotted him and brought him to the announcement center.

Joy and Reflection

Madhav returned to his tent, the family still shaken but full of relief and happiness. The fair, which brought him moments of spiritual connection, also tested his resilience. But amidst the chaos and confusion, they found a way to get back together. The next day, Madhav and his family returned to the river bank, not to bathe again but to give thanks.

The Ganga, in all its glory, flowed peacefully. The Ganga is a reminder that even amidst the world's largest crowd, a greater force was at work. Guiding him in his journey of faith. The Maha Kumbh Mela has left an indelible mark on the heart of Madhav for its religious significance and profound experiences blending awe, faith, joy and unity.

"Even in the darkest moments of uncertainty, hope can shine through like a beacon, guiding us to the miracle we least expect."

15

Madhav's Journey Through the Legal Labyrinth

While working in the Personnel Department, Madhav soon realized that if he wanted to grow in his career, gaining knowledge of law was essential. As an officer in the Human Resources department, Madhav frequently dealt with situations involving labor laws, worker rights, and disputes—all of which required a solid understanding of the legal framework. His desire to pursue formal legal education grew stronger, and the idea of enrolling in an LLB program took root.

The Determined Man

Madhav was known for his unwavering determination and commitment to everything he set his mind to. After facing several challenges in trying to balance his demanding job and academic aspirations, he finally decided to take the plunge and enroll in the LLB evening course at Allahabad University. Despite the course running two years behind schedule due to administrative delays, Madhav's resolve remained unshaken. He was ready to take on whatever challenges came his way.

The Campus Environment

Allahabad University, a historic institution renowned for producing eminent leaders, lawyers, and judges, had an atmosphere brimming with intellectual energy and political activity. The campus was lively, though often chaotic, with a constant buzz of debates and discussions. The LLB evening classes were attended by a diverse group of students, many of whom, like Madhav, were professionals seeking to advance their careers.

What surprised Madhav the most was the casual attitude of many of his fellow students. Most attended classes simply to meet the minimum attendance requirements, showing little interest in lectures or legal discussions. Some students were more engaged in campus politics than their studies, frequently skipping classes to participate in student union elections, protests, and sometimes even clashes between rival factions. Madhav found this lack of academic focus disappointing, especially given the serious nature of the subject matter.

A Journey of Balance and Determination

Despite the distractions around him, Madhav was determined to succeed. He took on the responsibility of managing a demanding full-time job during the day while diligently studying for his LLB in the evening. He understood the importance of passing exams on time and acquiring a thorough understanding of the law for his career advancement. His dedication did not go unnoticed by his professors, who, like him, were often frustrated by the indifference shown by many of the students in his class.

Madhav's journey through the legal labyrinth was not without its challenges, but his unwavering commitment to his goals kept him on track. Through every difficulty, he remained focused on his purpose, determined to make his mark in the field of law and human resources.

Clashes and Disruptions

The tension that had been brewing on campus for weeks finally reached its breaking point. Student union leaders, representing various factions, were at odds with the dean of the university. What had begun as a disagreement over an administrative decision soon escalated into a full-blown confrontation. Enraged students gathered in large numbers, shouting slogans and demanding the resignation of the dean.

As the situation spiraled out of control, clashes erupted between students and university officials. The atmosphere on campus became charged with hostility. Groups of students, divided by their political affiliations, engaged in violent fighting. Overwhelmed by the intensity of the unrest, the administration was forced to close the university indefinitely. Classes were suspended for more than a month, disrupting the academic schedule.

Madhav at a Crossroads

Madhav found himself at a crossroads. He was already struggling to balance his dual responsibilities of work and study. The sudden suspension of classes only intensified his frustration. The constant political drama on campus, the apathy of his peers, and the uncertainty surrounding when classes would resume began to take a toll on him. At times, it felt as though the odds were stacked against him.

The thought of abandoning his LLB program crept into his mind. The path ahead seemed more uncertain with each passing day, and the pressure to continue seemed overwhelming.

A Turning Point

One evening, as Madhav sat in his small apartment, he received an unexpected call from Dr. Sinha, one of his professors. Dr. Sinha was a renowned figure in the field of legal studies, known not only for his expertise but also for his commitment to meditation. Realizing that Madhav was on the verge of giving up, Dr. Sinha invited him to his office the following day.

During their meeting, Dr. Sinha spoke passionately about the significance of legal education—not just for a career in law, but for understanding the dynamics of society. He shared personal stories of his own struggles and the challenges he faced as a young man. Dr. Sinha explained how his legal knowledge had helped him navigate difficult situations and how the judiciary played a crucial role in maintaining the balance of power in a democracy.

The Spark of Change

Madhav listened intently as Dr. Sinha emphasized the importance of judges, legal experts, and individuals who stand for justice and fairness in society. Dr. Sinha's words resonated deeply with Madhav. As the professor spoke, Madhav began to understand the transformative power of legal knowledge—not only for professional development but also for personal empowerment.

The idea of abandoning his studies suddenly seemed like giving up on a lifelong dream. The frustration and uncertainty that had clouded his mind began to fade, replaced by a renewed sense of purpose.

Grateful for the professor's wisdom and guidance, Madhav made a firm decision that he would complete his LLB, no matter how challenging the road ahead might be.

The Final Push

With the university closed, Madhav decided to seize the opportunity to prepare for his exams. He immersed himself in legal textbooks, case studies, and past question papers. His daily routine included work during the day followed by hours of self-study in the evening. He reached out to professors who were willing to guide him through the complex topics of constitutional law, criminal law, and contracts. Despite distractions on campus, Madhav's dedication never faltered. His professors, recognizing his commitment, provided him with additional coaching sessions, offering invaluable insights into the legal system, the functioning of the judiciary, and the individual's role in upholding justice.

During this time, Madhav also befriended like-minded students who shared his passion for law. He formed a small study group where they discussed legal concepts, debated case laws, and visited local courts to observe real-life proceedings. These experiences deepened Madhav's understanding of the practical aspects of law and further strengthened his commitment to succeed.

The Importance of Legal Knowledge

When the university reopened and classes resumed, Madhav felt more confident than ever. He no longer felt overwhelmed by the challenges on campus; instead, he saw them as opportunities to grow and learn. The student union rivalry, campus disruptions, and the indifference of his peers no longer had any effect on him. Madhav had learned to focus on his goal without getting distracted by the chaos around him.

Madhav worked tirelessly during his final year. His dedication paid off as he excelled in his examinations, earning praise from his professors. When the results were declared, Madhav had passed the LLB course in one go, a feat that many students failed to achieve after multiple attempts. This degree was not just an academic achievement but a testament to his perseverance, discipline, and determination.

Conclusion

Madhav's journey at Allahabad University was far from easy. Political unrest, the indifference of his peers, and the challenges of balancing work and studies tested him in ways he had never imagined. Yet, through it all, he remained focused on his goal. His legal education became more than just a professional necessity; it transformed into a journey of self-discovery, resilience, and personal growth.

The LLB degree opened new doors for Madhav in his career. His enhanced understanding of labor laws, contracts, and the legal framework made him an invaluable asset at ITI Limited. His colleagues and superiors praised his legal expertise, and soon, he found himself handling complex legal matters with confidence. Most importantly, Madhav had learned that no matter how difficult the path may be, dedication and perseverance would always lead to success.

"Success is not defined by the ease of the journey, but by the strength to persevere through every challenge. Dedication, resilience, and unwavering focus will always turn obstacles into opportunities."

16

A Bundle of Joy

Madhav, a personnel officer at ITI Limited in Naini, followed a predictable daily routine. Every day, he commuted to the office by company bus, facing a world filled with meetings, labor disputes, and the demanding task of managing personnel. His life had become a seamless blend of the mundane, and he had long since adapted to the rhythm of his work. But little did Madhav know, this routine was about to take an unexpected turn.

A Surprising News at Home

One evening, after a long day at work, Madhav reached home as usual. However, as soon as he stepped inside, he sensed a change in the air. His mother, who always greeted him with a calm smile, was now beaming with joy. Her face radiated a happiness that Madhav had not seen in a long time.

Confused but curious, Madhav asked her, "Why are you so happy today?"

His mother signaled him to sit down. With a gentle, loving smile, she shared the life-changing news: Madhav was going to be a father. The words hung in the air, and for a moment, the world seemed to stop. His wife, Sandhya, was expecting their first child. A wave of emotions surged through him—excitement, joy, and disbelief, all mixing together in one overwhelming rush. The day he had dreamed of for so long had finally arrived.

After the initial shock, Madhav went to meet Sandhya. She was resting, and when she saw him, she smiled shyly, her face glowing with joy. Sitting beside her, he took her hand in his, feeling a deep connection as he realized that their lives were about to change in ways he never could have imagined.

Preparing for the Journey

The following week was a whirlwind of doctor's visits, check-ups, and a new sense of responsibility. The first visit to the doctor was filled with anticipation and excitement. The doctor gave them helpful advice—ensuring that Sandhya's health was carefully looked after, both physically and emotionally. "A healthy mother leads to a healthy child," the doctor emphasized. He instructed them to follow a healthy diet, get plenty of rest, and prioritize emotional well-being.

Regular check-ups became a part of Madhav and Sandhya's routine. Every visit reassured them that their baby's growth and health were progressing smoothly. Despite the challenges of pregnancy, Sandhya's joy was evident, though, like any expectant mother, she had her moments of worry. Late at night, she would wake up, her concerns about the delivery process lingering in her mind.

Madhav, ever calm and reassuring, would hold her hand, offering words of comfort. "Everything will be fine," he would say. "You're strong, and we're in this together. We'll make it through."

Through every step, they were united in their anticipation of the journey ahead, ready to embrace the beautiful changes that were unfolding in their lives.

The Day Arrives

The months passed quickly, filled with anticipation and preparation for the new arrival. Sandhya's belly grew bigger, and along with it, Madhav's excitement increased. The two spent hours discussing baby names, imagining what their child would look like, and dreaming about the future. On the morning of September 12, the day began like any other. As Madhav left for work, he kissed Sandhya goodbye. Last night, she had felt some discomfort, but neither of them expected the baby to arrive so soon. Madhav completed his usual tasks at the office, but his thoughts kept wandering back to Sandhya. Something felt different about that day, though he couldn't understand why.

Then came the call.

The Call

It was her father on the phone, his voice shaking with excitement. "Madhav, come to the hospital immediately! Sandhya has given birth to a beautiful baby girl!" For a moment, Madhav stood still, his heart racing. A wave of joy, shock, and disbelief washed over him. His daughter had arrived while he was still at work. Without a second thought, he rushed to the hospital, his mind racing with the thought of meeting his daughter for the first time.

First Meeting His Daughter

When Madhav arrived at the hospital, he saw his father holding the newborn, wrapped in a soft blanket. The little baby looked delicate, serene, and beautiful. As his father approached, Madhav's heart swelled with emotions, a proud smile spreading across his face. "You're here," his father said, his voice full of pride and love. Madhav gently took the newborn in his arms for the first time, his hands trembling. The moment he held her, time seemed to stop. She was so small, so fragile, weighing just 2.7 kg. Her soft, pink skin glowed with the light of life. Her tiny fingers were slightly curled, and her peaceful, calm face betrayed no hint of the chaos that had just unfolded. Madhav's eyes welled up with tears as he gazed at his daughter. He had never felt anything like this before—tremendous love, overwhelming responsibility, and the indescribable joy of holding his child for the first time. He couldn't control his tears. His father, seeing his son overcome with emotion, smiled and placed a comforting hand on his shoulder, offering silent support. Madhav, tears streaming down his face, turned to his father, bowed, and touched his feet in a gesture of deep respect and gratitude. "Thank you, Babuji," he whispered, his voice thick with emotion. His father blessed him, pride shining in his eyes.

A Moment of Peace

After holding his daughter in his arms, an experience that would stay with him forever, Madhav walked over to Sandhya, who was resting in bed. She was exhausted but radiated peace and satisfaction. After enduring long hours of labor, the sight of her husband and daughter together made all the pain worthwhile. Madhav knelt beside her, gently placing their daughter in her arms. Sandhya smiled, a single tear rolling down her cheek as she gazed into Madhav's eyes. Madhav whispered softly, "She's beautiful... I can't take my eyes off this little miracle we've created together." Sandhya nodded, her heart overflowing with love as she cradled their newborn daughter close. Madhav, too, couldn't stop marveling at their baby—her soft skin, tiny fingers, and serene expression. He knew, in that moment, that his life had changed forever. His heart swelled with the joy of becoming a father, and no words could express the depth of his emotions.

A New Chapter Begins

That night, Madhav stayed by Sandhya's side, watching over his wife and daughter. His world had grown infinitely larger, filled with new responsibilities, love, and endless possibilities. The arrival of their daughter had brought a happiness into their lives that they had never imagined. Madhav knew that this was just the beginning of a beautiful new chapter in their lives.

"Parenthood is a journey where love and responsibility intertwine, transforming every moment into a new beginning, and every challenge into a blessing."

17

The Golden Years: A Story of Health, Tradition, and Community in Allahabad

The ancient city of Allahabad, renowned for its confluence of rivers and rich spiritual heritage, was the backdrop to a fulfilling chapter in the lives of Madhav's parents. After retiring from the Indian Army, Madhav's father, Colonel B. Dwivedi, embraced a new phase of life with vigor and purpose. A disciplined and respected man, he shifted his focus from national defense to personal well-being, spiritual health, and community service. Alongside his wife, Rajeshwari Devi, he dedicated his post-retirement years to nurturing a community of like-minded senior citizens. Together, they wove a tapestry of tradition, health, and mutual care that became an enduring legacy.

A Life of Discipline and Purpose

Colonel Dwivedi's life had been defined by discipline and service. Even after retirement, he upheld the values of routine and order as vital tools for maintaining physical and mental health. Inspired by his military background, he approached this new chapter with the same dedication that had characterized his career. His vision extended beyond personal growth to the well-being of his community, particularly its senior members, who often struggled with a lack of purpose and motivation.

The Formation of a Senior Citizens' Community

Recognizing a need for connection and activity among retirees in his neighborhood, Colonel Dwivedi took the initiative to form a senior citizens' group. His leadership quickly attracted over 25 members from various professions, including schoolteachers and retired civil servants. These individuals came together with a shared purpose: to lead a meaningful and enriching life.

Each morning, the group visited a nearby temple to chant ancient shlokas, including the **Sunderkand** and **Hanuman Chalisa** from the *Ramcharitmanas*. These rituals were more than spiritual practices; they were opportunities for self-reflection, inner peace, and the strengthening of communal bonds. Colonel Dwivedi's efforts transformed mundane mornings into sacred gatherings, filled with purpose and harmony.

Evenings of Reflection and Wisdom

Every evening at 4 p.m., the group assembled in a lush neighborhood park. Surrounded by the laughter of children playing cricket, joggers circling the track, and young couples enjoying moments of leisure, the senior citizens created their own vibrant corner of intellectual and spiritual exploration.

Sitting in a circle on the soft grass, the group engaged in discussions on religious and philosophical topics drawn from texts such as the *Mahabharata*, *Ramayana*, and the *Vedas*. Each day, one or two members delivered a speech on a chosen topic, sparking lively debates and shared reflections. Whether exploring the moral dilemmas of the *Mahabharata* or the devotion depicted in the *Ramayana*, these discussions were rich in insight and wisdom.

The atmosphere was marked by respect, empathy, and camaraderie. Every voice was valued, and no perspective was ignored. The group's intellectual exercises kept their minds sharp, spirits high, and friendships deep. This tradition continued for over 18 years, becoming an integral part of Colonel Dwivedi's life and a cherished routine for all participants.

Legacy of a Life Well-Lived

Colonel Dwivedi's leadership and vision created a community that thrived on mutual care, shared learning, and spiritual growth. His ability to bring people together and inspire them to live with purpose left an indelible mark on his neighborhood. Through the rituals of morning prayers and evening discourses, he and his group of senior citizens exemplified the essence of healthy, meaningful living in their golden years.

The story of Colonel B. Dwivedi and his community in Allahabad serves as a timeless reminder of the importance of discipline, tradition, and connection in leading a fulfilling life. It is a testament to the power of one individual's determination to transform lives and foster a sense of belonging, even in the later stages of life.

Morning Rituals: A Journey of Devotion and Community

Madhav's father might have led the people as a community figure, but his mother carved her own inspiring path. She was an early riser, a trait that defined her disciplined lifestyle. Along with a group of women, mostly housewives like her, she embraced the dawn with purpose and devotion.

Every morning, Madhav's mother and her companions made their way to the sacred river Ganga for their daily bath. The Ganga, revered for centuries as a holy river, symbolized not just physical cleansing but also spiritual renewal. What began as a small circle of women eventually grew to over a dozen participants, all eager to start their day with the river's transformative embrace.

The cool waters of the Ganga, especially invigorating during winter, energized their bodies and minds. After the bath, the group gathered briefly for prayers, their voices harmonizing in devotion before returning home to prepare breakfast for their families.

This morning ritual was more than a routine; it was a celebration of friendship, community, and faith—a shared experience that brought meaning to their lives.

Evening Walks: Fitness and Fellowship

As the sun set and household chores were completed, Madhav's mother's group reconvened in the nearby park. This was the same place where the men of the community engaged in spiritual discussions.

The evening walk was not just an exercise; it was a moment to unwind, connect, and rejuvenate. Together, they strolled along the park pathways, sometimes in comfortable silence and other times chatting about their day.

Following Madhav's mother's example, the women took pride in maintaining their health and youthful spirits. These walks strengthened their bodies, nurtured their minds, and created lasting bonds. The park became a sanctuary where laughter, light conversation, and shared purpose flourished.

A Circle of Care: Strength in Togetherness

Both Madhav's father's senior citizens' group and his mother's women's group shared an admirable quality—unwavering support for one another.

If any member fell ill, others rallied around them with food, companionship, and help with daily tasks. They ensured no one felt isolated during challenging times. If a member missed a gathering due to a doctor's appointment or family obligation, they were updated and welcomed back with warmth the following day.

This sense of care and compassion extended far beyond their meetings. It wove into their everyday lives, creating a safety net of love and support. Each member took comfort in knowing they belonged to a group that genuinely cared about their well-being.

Legacy of Love and Resilience

Through her morning rituals, evening walks, and unwavering compassion, Madhav's mother exemplified strength, devotion, and community spirit. She not only shaped her own life but also inspired others to embrace health, faith, and friendship.

Her story is a testament to the power of small, meaningful actions—actions that build strong bonds, transform communities, and leave an enduring legacy of love and resilience.

As the years passed, Madhav's parents remained deeply involved in their respective community groups. With the responsibilities of raising children and earning a living behind them, they embraced a life of purpose and fulfillment.

Their days were filled with simple yet meaningful rituals: morning prayers, refreshing baths by the riverbank, stimulating philosophical discussions, and serene evening walks. These routines became cherished habits, not just for them but for the entire community.

A Community Built on Mutual Respect

The community, guided by cooperation and mutual respect, thrived under the leadership of senior citizens like Madhav's father. Together, they took turns organizing events, arranging temple visits, and planning picnics. Meanwhile, Madhav's mother and her women's group often hosted special religious ceremonies and intimate gatherings in each other's homes.

This harmonious coexistence served as an inspiring example for younger generations. Through their actions, they taught their children and grandchildren the profound value of staying active—both physically and mentally—and embracing empathy, cooperation, and self-care.

A Legacy of Wellness and Happiness

Madhav often marveled at his parents' vibrancy and zest for life. Their unwavering commitment to physical and spiritual health allowed them to thrive well into their senior years.

Simple Routines with Profound Impact

For them, routines were more than mere traditions; they were sources of joy, meaning, and connection. The day would start with a group of senior citizens gathering for a sacred morning bath in the Ganga, followed by enriching conversations and an evening stroll.

In these simple yet profound rituals, Madhav's parents and their community discovered the true essence of life: a balance of health, spiritual contentment, and deep, meaningful relationships.

Inspiring Future Generations

The legacy they created was one of wellness and happiness. Their lifestyle inspired all who knew them, instilling a sense of purpose and harmony that would resonate for generations. By demonstrating how to live a fulfilling life through cooperation and care, Madhav's parents left an indelible mark on their family and community.

"True fulfillment lies in simple joys, shared purpose, and the harmony of caring hearts—where every moment becomes a legacy of wellness and every action an inspiration for generations to come."

18

The Turning Point

In response to the unrest in the ITI colony,Bengluru the company's management took decisive action. Madhav, known for his dedication and sense of responsibility, was entrusted with the task of restoring order and ensuring the security of the township. Although it seemed like a daunting challenge, Madhav was determined to bring about a change.

His first step was to consult with the local police and top management. He emphasized the seriousness of the situation and presented a comprehensive plan to eliminate the anti-social elements that had taken root in the colony. The local police pledged their support, recognizing that a safe township was in everyone's best interests. Together, they devised a plan to implement effective security measures and restore a sense of control.

Fortifying Security

Security personnel were deployed immediately, and strict rules were enforced. The once-open gates were now closed, leaving only a few entrances. Security guards were stationed at these gates to monitor the movement of all visitors. People not residing in the colony were denied entry.

The pandemic era presented an unexpected opportunity for Madhav to strengthen security further. With the entire world focused on health and safety, he seized the moment. Most of the colony's gates were permanently closed, allowing access only through a single entrance. This strategic control of movement ensured that the flow of people in and out of the township could be strictly monitored.

This decision proved to be a turning point. Gradually, the chaotic environment began to improve, and the township started to regain its sense of order.

A New Dawn

As security improved, the overall atmosphere in the township began to change. Residents, once living in fear, now walked freely, without worry. Families strolled through the gardens, and children played in safety. What had once been a community on the verge of collapse was slowly starting to recover.

Vacant and abandoned quarters, which had once attracted rioters, were gradually rehabilitated. The company initiated a renovation project, transforming neglected spaces into welcoming homes. The overgrown gardens, a symbol of the colony's decline, were revived. Landscapers were brought in to restore the greenery, plant flowers, and trim the hedges, bringing back the beauty of the surroundings.

As the physical environment improved, so did the sense of community. Residents, once isolated, began reconnecting. Neighborhood groups formed, and social gatherings returned. Small festivals, cultural programs, and evening get-togethers were organized. The vibrant community spirit, which had once defined the township, was revived in full force.

A Thriving Economy

As the environment in the colony improved, economic prosperity followed suit. Local businesses, which had suffered during the township's turbulent times, began to flourish once again. Small shops and vendors reopened, providing essential goods and services to residents. The township's market square, once quiet and deserted, was now buzzing with activity. Residents who had initially considered moving away decided to stay, drawn by the new security arrangements. New families started moving in, attracted by the township's newfound reputation for cleanliness and order.

The population grew, and with it, economic development flourished. The township's schools experienced a rise in enrollment, as families felt confident that their children were being raised in a safe and nurturing environment. The transformation was nothing short of remarkable. From the depths of despair, the township had risen, largely thanks to Madhav's unwavering commitment to restoring order. What was once a place of fear and uncertainty had now become a symbol of prosperity and harmony.

The Legacy of Change

Madhav's tireless efforts left an enduring legacy. His dream of a safe, clean, and vibrant colony had finally become a reality. Residents now felt secure in their homes. The colony was immaculate, its gardens well-maintained, and the streets orderly. The inhabitants of the colony were now able to enjoy peace without fear.

The safety measures introduced during the pandemic continued to have a long-lasting impact. Having a single main gate ensured strict control over who entered the township, while local police and security personnel maintained a constant presence, keeping miscreants at bay. More importantly, the community regained its sense of pride. The settlement that had once been on the verge of collapse was now a model of good governance and prosperity.

Families enjoyed spending time in the well-maintained gardens, socialized with neighbors, and felt assured that their children were growing up in a safe and nurturing environment. The township had been transformed into a hub of peace, security, and economic growth. It stood as a testament to the power of community, determination, and strong leadership.

"Every step you take, no matter how small, brings you closer to the person you are destined to become. Keep moving forward, for greatness lies in persistence."

19

Title: A Holi to Remember: Madhav and Santosh's Township Celebration

Madhav and Santosh, both employees at the same company, lived in Company Township. Holi, the vibrant festival of colors, was always a time of celebration, and this year, the two friends decided to do something extraordinary. They envisioned an event that would bring everyone together, creating a festival where both young and old could celebrate the true spirit of Holi.

The Dream: A Celebration for All Ages

Known for their leadership and active involvement in community programs, Madhav and Santosh dreamed of organizing a grand cultural festival for the entire township. This Holi, they envisioned something beyond just color and fun; they wanted to bridge the generational gap that existed within the colony. They gathered a team of five trusted friends, each equally enthusiastic about making this idea a reality. Their vision was simple - to create an event that united people of all ages, fostering connection and harmony.

The Planning Begins

During their first meeting, the team laid out their plans. It was decided that the celebration wouldn't be limited to the current residents of the township. They would also invite retired officers who had once contributed greatly to the company. Many of these retirees had settled in Bengaluru after their retirement, and the team felt it would be the perfect opportunity to honor them by including them in the celebration. This would add a sense of importance to the event and allow the younger generation to interact with the seniors, learning from their experiences.

A small token amount was collected from each house to cover the expenses for decorations, food, and entertainment. Word of the event spread quickly through the colony, and the excitement grew. For many, it would be the first time in years that such a large-scale event was being organized. The children were especially thrilled, and a cultural program was planned featuring songs, dances, and even a live round of Antakshari. Parents busily rehearsed with their children, and the atmosphere was electric with anticipation.

The Dilemma: A Question of Generations

As Holi drew closer, the planning team faced a dilemma. Some residents were hesitant about inviting the retired officers, questioning whether it would change the nature of the event. Concerns arose that the presence of senior officials might turn the celebration from a lively, informal event into something more structured and formal. Some feared this would lessen the fun and spontaneity of the celebration.

However, Madhav and Santosh believed it was essential to involve the retired officers. Holi, after all, is a festival that symbolizes unity and togetherness, and what better way to promote that than by bringing different generations together? They discussed the issue with their team and, after much thought, reached a consensus. The retired officers would be invited, but participation would be entirely optional. It was important that everyone felt comfortable, and there would be no obligation to attend.

The Invitations: A Celebration of Choice

Invitations were sent out to the retired officers with the understanding that their presence would be welcomed, but it would be entirely up to them whether to attend. Some seniors accepted eagerly, excited to reconnect with former colleagues and share the joy of the festival with the younger generation. Others, however, politely declined, preferring to spend the day in a more relaxed setting.

A Colorful and Unified Celebration

As the day of Holi arrived, the township was transformed into a colorful canvas. The energy was palpable, with people of all ages coming together to celebrate. The children performed their cultural program, and the seniors, though few, participated in the festivities, sharing their wisdom and stories. The event was a beautiful blend of generations, each adding their unique flavor to the celebration.

In the end, Madhav and Santosh's vision had come to life, proving that a festival of colors could also be a festival of unity. It was a Holi to remember, one that bridged gaps, created lasting memories, and brought the community together in the true spirit of the festival.

The Event Unfolds

The day of the event arrived, and the entire colony buzzed with excitement. The streets and central grounds were beautifully decorated for the ceremony, setting a vibrant atmosphere. A stage had been set up for the children's performances, and tables were arranged for the dinner that would follow. As the program began, the colony was filled with laughter and joy. The children dazzled the audience with their performances, showcasing dances and songs that celebrated the rich and diverse culture of India.

Antakshari, the popular musical game, became the highlight of the evening. Teams competed with great enthusiasm, creating a friendly yet competitive atmosphere. The cultural program was a huge success, delighting both seniors and juniors alike. But amidst the celebration, there was a growing tension. Two men, Rajesh and Arvind, who harbored a long-standing personal grudge, were present at the event. Both were influential figures in the colony, but their egos often clashed, creating an uneasy atmosphere whenever they were in the same place. Despite their differences, they had both chosen to participate in the event, each determined not to let the other steal the limelight.

As the evening wore on, their minor disagreements began to escalate. What started as a simple difference of opinion regarding the seating arrangement soon turned into a heated argument. Voices were raised, and the joyful mood of the event began to change. The two men stood face to face, shouting at each other in front of the audience. Bystanders attempted to intervene, but their efforts only seemed to fuel the fire.

Madhav Steps In

Realizing that the argument was beginning to overshadow the entire event, Madhav immediately stepped in. He knew both Rajesh and Arvind well and understood that their conflict was driven more by personal ego than any real issue at hand. Remaining calm and composed, Madhav approached the two men and began speaking softly to them.

With conviction, Madhav reminded them that Holi was a festival of colors, happiness, and unity. He urged them to resolve their differences—not for their own sake, but for the sake of those who had gathered to enjoy the evening. Both Rajesh and Arvind began to listen attentively. Madhav continued, emphasizing that the event was meant to bring everyone together in joy. He reminded them of the respect they commanded within the colony and encouraged them to set aside their differences for one night and fully enjoy the festivities.

There was a brief pause, and for a moment, it seemed as though the tension might reignite. But Madhav's calm demeanor and appeal to their sense of responsibility began to soften both men. Slowly, the fire in their eyes dimmed. They exchanged a glance, and the intensity of the argument began to fade.

Rajesh, now more composed, extended his hand towards Arvind and apologized for overreacting. He admitted that he had become carried away. Arvind, in turn, accepted the apology with a handshake. The crowd, which had been anxiously watching the confrontation, breathed a collective sigh of relief.

The atmosphere, once again, was filled with warmth and joy, as the event continued without further disruption. Thanks to Madhav's timely intervention, the celebration was restored to its intended spirit of unity and happiness.

A Night to Remember

With the debate resolved, the atmosphere soon returned to a celebratory mood. The final performance of the evening received a standing ovation, and the dinner that followed was a great success. The food was delicious, and the residents were laughing freely and sharing stories. The retired officers, who had initially been hesitant, expressed their happiness at participating in the event. For many, it was an opportunity to reconnect with old friends and remember the colony's golden days. Madhav, Santosh, and their team were widely praised for their efforts in organizing such a successful event.

The event was not only a celebration of Holi but also an occasion that brought the community together. Despite the near-disruption caused by the initial confusion and debate about inviting seniors, the evening ended on a high note. This was the first time such an event had been organized in the colony, and the residents were looking forward to more such events in the future.

As night approached, Madhav reflected on the evening. This incident had shown him the importance of coordination, communication, and the delicate balance of managing egos and personal differences. But most importantly, it strengthened his belief in the power of community. Holi was a festival of unity, and with their efforts, Madhav and Santosh had successfully reminded everyone of that spirit. The colony residents had experienced a night of joy, laughter, and togetherness—a memorable Holi.

"Unity is born from the shared moments of joy and togetherness. When we set aside differences and work towards a common goal, we create memories that remind us of the power of community."

20

Madhav's Challenge at the Corporate Office: A Battle Over Employment Age Limits

Madhav, an experienced and skilled negotiator in labor disputes, was recently transferred to the corporate office of a large and reputed public sector undertaking with branches across the country. Known for his ability to tackle challenging cases, Madhav now faced a matter of unprecedented scale and sensitivity. The issue on his desk would significantly impact the company's employees, senior management, and its long-term operational strategies.

The case at hand was the controversial ruling by the Karnataka High Court, which mandated an increase in the retirement age of employees from 58 to 60 years.

The High Court Ruling

For years, the company's employees had been fighting to raise their retirement age, aligning it with other public sector organizations. They cited labor laws, service conditions, and the company's standing orders to substantiate their claim.

The employees' counsel argued that with changing economic realities and increasing life expectancy, the company's retirement policy was outdated and discriminatory. After prolonged deliberations, the Karnataka High Court ruled in favor of the employees, directing the company to implement the change.

While this decision was a victory for the employees, it presented a serious challenge for the company's management. Extending the retirement age would not only disrupt the carefully planned workforce structure but also impose significant financial burdens. The ripple effects included complications in future recruitment and potential repercussions for the morale of the company's executives.

The Corporate Dilemma

Madhav's expertise in handling labor disputes made him the ideal choice to address this complex issue. However, the situation was far from straightforward.

The High Court's decision posed a multifaceted dilemma:

- **Impact on Labor Laws and Policies:** The company's standing orders, crafted through years of negotiation between management and labor unions, explicitly stated the retirement age as 58. Altering this would challenge the integrity of the company's internal policies.

- **Financial and Strategic Concerns:** Extending the retirement age would strain the company's financial resources and disrupt its long-term workforce planning. The move would delay the recruitment of new talent and affect future operational strategies.
- **Divided Leadership:** The company's top management was split on the issue. While some leaders advocated accepting the High Court's decision to maintain harmony with employees, others, including Madhav, argued that the company had grounds to appeal the ruling. Challenging the decision, however, risked further straining relations with the workforce.

Madhav's Role and Strategy

Madhav understood the gravity of his responsibility. He needed to balance legal, financial, and human factors while ensuring the company's long-term interests were protected.

His approach involved:

- **Engaging Stakeholders:** Madhav prioritized open communication with employees, unions, and management to address concerns and minimize friction.
- **Analyzing Legal Options:** He reviewed the High Court ruling and the company's standing orders to determine the viability of an appeal.
- **Mitigating Financial Impact:** Madhav worked with the finance team to assess the monetary implications and identify potential measures to offset costs.

- **Safeguarding Morale:** Recognizing the importance of employee morale, he sought solutions that would foster trust and uphold the company's reputation.

Conclusion

Madhav's challenge was not merely a battle over retirement age but a test of his leadership and problem-solving abilities. The case highlighted the delicate balance between honoring judicial rulings, respecting employee demands, and preserving the organization's operational integrity.

As Madhav strategized his next steps, he knew that this decision would shape the future of the company and set a precedent for public sector undertakings across the nation.

Preparing for the Supreme Court

The company, facing a critical legal challenge, decided to file an appeal in the Supreme Court, seeking a stay on the High Court's decision. Implementation of the decision would be put on hold until the Supreme Court could thoroughly review the case. Without the moratorium, the company would have been compelled to immediately raise the retirement age—an action that would be difficult to reverse.

Formulating the Legal Strategy

Madhav, taking the lead in crafting the company's legal strategy, understood the high stakes involved. Aware of the risks, he engaged the services of an experienced senior lawyer, renowned for expertise in labor law and a strong track record in Supreme Court litigation. However, the magnitude of the case demanded more than just a skilled legal expert.

Madhav and the company's top management agreed to approach the Solicitor General of India, the country's second-highest legal officer, to represent their case. Madhav knew this was no small feat—the Solicitor General's office only accepted matters of national significance. Securing an appointment was itself a challenge, but Madhav managed to do so, demonstrating the gravity of the situation.

Nervous Beginnings: Meeting the Solicitor General

The day of the meeting arrived, and Madhav, accompanied by a senior company executive with prior experience in legal matters, entered the Solicitor General's chambers. The air was heavy with anticipation. Madhav, though seasoned in labor disputes and legal procedures, found himself uneasy. Presenting the case to such a distinguished legal stalwart felt daunting.

The Solicitor General, a calm yet imposing figure with decades of experience, greeted them with a firm handshake. Madhav's nervousness was evident as he began presenting the company's concerns regarding the High Court ruling. His voice trembled slightly, reflecting the weight of responsibility he carried.

Building Confidence: A Stronger Argument Emerges

As Madhav delved deeper into the legal intricacies, his confidence grew. He articulated the company's position with clarity and precision, emphasizing:

- **The Legally Binding Nature of the Standing Orders:** Madhav explained how the company's

Standing Orders had been negotiated and agreed upon with labor unions over the years. These orders were legally binding, and altering the retirement age without due process would set a perilous precedent.

- **Potential Flood of Legal Challenges:** Madhav highlighted the broader implications of the High Court ruling. Officials excluded from the original case could now file similar petitions, potentially leading to a surge in legal challenges and a significant financial burden for the company.
- **Need for a Supreme Court Review:** He stressed the importance of a stay on the High Court judgment to allow the Supreme Court to examine the case thoroughly. Rushing into implementation could create irreversible consequences.

A Decisive Moment

As Madhav concluded, the Solicitor General listened intently, occasionally interjecting with pointed questions that tested the strength of the arguments. Madhav answered with composure, demonstrating his deep understanding of the issues at hand. By the end of the meeting, the Solicitor General acknowledged the gravity of the matter and agreed to consider representing the company's case.

This pivotal interaction not only reinforced the company's resolve but also set the stage for a high-stakes legal battle that could shape its future. For Madhav, it was a moment of both personal and professional growth—a testament to his dedication and ability to rise to the occasion when it mattered most.

The Solicitor General's Strategy

After listening attentively to Madhav's arguments, the Solicitor General nodded thoughtfully, visibly impressed by the detailed groundwork Madhav had prepared. Despite Madhav's initial nervousness, it was evident that the case had been meticulously planned. Recognizing the potential merit, the Solicitor General agreed to take up the case, offering his legal expertise to further refine the arguments.

He outlined a clear strategy to be presented before the Supreme Court, emphasizing the service conditions outlined in the company's standing orders. The Solicitor General argued that the High Court's decision had undermined these legally binding agreements. He pointed out that any changes to the terms of service should have been the result of negotiations involving all stakeholders, not a unilateral judicial decision.

He also highlighted the far-reaching consequences of the judgment, warning of potential legal chaos if the ruling were to stand. Specifically, he noted the risk it posed to company executives and the precedent it might set for similar cases in the future. With the Solicitor General's support and strategic insights, Madhav left the meeting feeling a renewed sense of relief and confidence. For the first time, he believed they stood a real chance of securing a stay on the High Court's decision.

The Supreme Court Hearing

A few weeks later, the case was scheduled for a hearing before the Supreme Court. The company's top management placed its trust in Madhav and the legal team to represent its interests effectively. While Madhav still felt a twinge of nervousness, his earlier meeting with the Solicitor General had instilled in him a sense of preparedness and calm determination.

Arguments from the Employees' Counsel

On the day of the hearing, the courtroom wastense with anticipation. The senior counsel representing the employees opened the arguments, passionately defending the High Court's decision. The counsel argued that the company's refusal to increase the retirement age was both unjust and discriminatory. They emphasized that changing economic conditions and increased life expectancy had reshaped employment expectations, making the extension of the retirement age a reasonable and necessary demand.

The Solicitor General's Counterarguments

When it was the company's turn, the Solicitor General took the lead with a commanding presence. He began by meticulously outlining the company's standing orders, arguing that these were legally binding agreements that could not be altered arbitrarily. While acknowledging the legitimacy of the employees' concerns, he asserted that changes to employment conditions should come through legislative or administrative processes—not judicial intervention.

The Solicitor General further underscored the broader implications of the High Court's decision. He warned that if the ruling were allowed to stand, it could lead to a cascade of legal challenges from other employee groups, including executives, potentially causing significant financial strain and operational disruptions for the company.

A Glimmer of Hope

As the Solicitor General concluded his arguments, it was clear that his methodical and precise approach had made an impact. Madhav, sitting among the legal team, felt a surge of hope. The Solicitor General's representation had not only reinforced the company's position but also highlighted the broader legal and operational risks posed by the High Court's judgment.

With the hearing concluded, Madhav felt cautiously optimistic. The company had presented a robust case, and now all they could do was wait for the Supreme Court's decision.

The Supreme Court's Decision: A Temporary Relief

After hearing compelling arguments from both sides, the Supreme Court judges retired to their chambers to deliberate. The courtroom buzzed with tension, each side anxiously awaiting the verdict. Hours later, the presiding judge returned with a crucial decision.

The Supreme Court granted the company a stay on the High Court's ruling, declaring that until the matter was thoroughly reviewed, the current retirement age would remain at 58 years. This ruling brought significant relief to the company, giving it valuable time to prepare for the full hearing.

Madhav's Leadership Shines Amidst Challenges

For Madhav, the interim victory was a testament to his exceptional leadership and ability to navigate complex challenges in corporate HR. Despite initial apprehensions, Madhav rose to the occasion, demonstrating resilience and strategic acumen.

The case was far from over, but the stay granted by the Supreme Court allowed the company to operate without the immediate threat of a policy overhaul. It was a pivotal moment that underscored Madhav's critical role in safeguarding the organization's future.

A New Chapter: Building Bridges with Employees

In the months that followed, the company took proactive steps to address employees' concerns. Leadership initiated constructive dialogues and negotiations to resolve the issue amicably.

Madhav led these discussions with newfound confidence, applying lessons learned during the legal battle. His efforts focused on balancing the company's operational goals with the employees' expectations, paving the way for a fair and sustainable resolution.

"True leadership shines in moments of adversity—when challenges demand courage, resilience, and the vision to turn setbacks into stepping stones for a brighter future."

21

Madhav's First Legal Battle as HR Head: A Journey Through the Jodhpur High Court

A Prestigious Assignment with Unexpected Challenges

Madhav, with his robust background in law and extensive experience in human resources, was recently transferred to the prestigious post of HR Head at the Network Systems (NS) Unit, a key division of a renowned public sector enterprise. Taking up this role was both an honor and a responsibility, but little did he know that his first major challenge would thrust him into a complex legal storm.

The Legal Quagmire: Casual Workers vs. The Company

At the heart of this storm was a long-standing dispute over the employment status of several contingent workers. These employees, appointed on a casual basis, had filed a writ petition in the Jodhpur High Court, demanding permanent employment. Their argument was simple yet compelling: many of them had been working with the company for over a decade, and their roles had evolved into essential functions. Some claimed they had been given verbal assurances by top management regarding regularization, but these promises never materialized.

The Workers' Standpoint

The workers' legal representatives argued that their prolonged service and critical contributions to the company had created a legitimate expectation of permanency. They alleged that the company's failure to regularize their employment was unjust and amounted to wrongful dismissal.

The Company's Counterarguments

On the other side, the company maintained a firm stance. The workers were hired strictly on a contingent basis with no explicit promise of permanency. From the company's perspective, the legal claims for regularization were baseless, as the employment agreements clearly outlined the temporary nature of their roles.

Years of Deadlock and Mounting Pressure

The case had been dragging on for years, with several hearings but little resolution. Local unions rallied behind the workers, amplifying the matter's sensitivity. The ongoing dispute garnered significant media attention, placing immense pressure on the company's HR department to find a swift and effective solution.

Madhav's Role in the Eye of the Storm

When Madhav assumed his role as HR Head, he inherited this deeply entrenched legal battle. Resolving the matter was not just a legal challenge but also a test of his leadership and problem-solving abilities. The stakes were high—ensuring justice for the workers while safeguarding the company's legal and financial interests.

A Roadmap to Resolution

Determined to tackle the issue head-on, Madhav began reviewing the case details meticulously. His legal expertise, combined with his strategic HR acumen, would be critical in navigating this complex situation. The journey through the Jodhpur High Court was bound to be challenging, but Madhav was prepared to turn this daunting battle into an opportunity to demonstrate resilience, fairness, and leadership.

Madhav's New Role: Shouldering Unexpected Responsibility

When Madhav joined as the HR head, he knew his role would involve complex challenges. However, he didn't anticipate being thrust into the middle of a high-stakes legal battle. Armed with a law degree, Madhav was tasked with overseeing the company's defense in an intricate case involving jurisdiction disputes, labor laws, and landmark precedents.

His first task was to collect all relevant documents, coordinate with the legal team, and ensure the company was fully prepared for the upcoming High Court hearing.

The stakes were high, as the court had set a new date for the final round of arguments. Madhav, determined to leave no stone unturned, traveled to Jodhpur with the company's top management, ready to support his team.

The Unexpected Strike: A Twist in the Tale

Upon reaching Jodhpur, Madhav received startling news: the lawyers had gone on strike. The legal team that had diligently represented the company for years could not attend the crucial hearing. This placed the company in a precarious situation.

The judges of the Jodhpur High Court, in a highly unusual move, decided to proceed with hearings despite the absence of lawyers. Madhav's senior officials, who accompanied him, were apprehensive. Facing the court without legal counsel seemed like an insurmountable challenge.

Madhav, though not a seasoned litigator, knew that skipping the hearing would mean forfeiting the company's right to defend itself. A judgment passed in their absence could have dire consequences. Despite his initial hesitation and nervousness, Madhav resolved to take the initiative.

Rising to the Occasion: Madhav's Brave Stand

Realizing the gravity of the situation, Madhav quickly gathered his thoughts. He had prepared meticulously, reviewing the company's position with legal advisors before the strike and studying labor laws that supported their defense. Armed with essential documents and a clear understanding of the arguments, he braced himself for one of the most challenging days of his career.

Walking into the courtroom, Madhav felt the weight of responsibility on his shoulders. Yet, he was determined to ensure the company's voice was heard. His courage and quick thinking transformed a potential disaster into a moment of resilience.

Lessons in Leadership

Madhav's experience highlighted the importance of adaptability, courage, and preparation in the face of unexpected challenges. While the strike and courtroom drama tested his mettle, his unwavering determination and willingness to step up earned him the respect of his team and the company's leadership.

Through this journey, Madhav proved that true leaders rise to the occasion, even in the most daunting circumstances.

Facing the Judge: Madhav's First Courtroom Experience

Madhav stepped into the courtroom with a mixture of fear and determination. This was his first time standing before a judge in a high-profile case, entirely on his own, without the safety net of legal counsel. The courtroom's formality and the weight of the occasion were daunting.

On one side stood the plaintiffs—the informal workers—bereft of their legal representation due to an ongoing strike. On the other side was Madhav, representing the company, alone yet resolute.

When the judge called the case and invited both sides to present their arguments, Madhav's heart raced. The stakes were enormous. A single misstep could not only derail his career but also cost the company a hefty sum in compensation if the decision went against them.

Taking a deep, steadying breath, Madhav stepped forward and began his argument.

Laying Out the Company's Case

Madhav started by setting out the facts with clarity and precision. He emphasized that the workers had been employed under casual contracts, which were explicitly outlined in their terms of employment. Producing detailed documentation, Madhav demonstrated that the employees had been fully aware of their casual status from the beginning and had signed the contracts acknowledging this.

To strengthen his case, Madhav cited previous rulings from high courts and the Supreme Court, where judgments in similar situations had favored companies. He argued that the company had acted within the legal framework and had not violated any workers' rights.

Madhav also tackled the issue of jurisdiction, explaining that the Jodhpur High Court was the appropriate venue for the case. He pointed out that the activists supporting the workers had misinterpreted the law in their appeal.

The judge listened intently, occasionally interjecting with questions to clarify specific points. Madhav's confidence grew with each answer he gave, noticing the judge's engagement and understanding of the company's position.

The Turning Point

After Madhav's initial presentation, the judge scheduled two additional hearings to examine the case thoroughly.

The plaintiffs attempted to present their arguments, but their case lacked the legal depth and substantiation that Madhav brought to the table. Their claims appeared inconsistent and poorly prepared, weakening their position significantly.

In the subsequent hearings, Madhav refined his arguments, focusing on the company's adherence to termination procedures. He demonstrated that due process had been followed meticulously and highlighted the absence of any legal standing for the plaintiffs to challenge their dismissals or demand permanent employment.

Victory in Sight

Madhav's meticulous preparation and unwavering determination began to bear fruit. By the final hearing, it was evident that the judge was leaning in favor of the company. Madhav's arguments, supported by legal precedents and documented evidence, had convincingly addressed every aspect of the case.

What started as an intimidating experience transformed into a testament to Madhav's resilience and legal acumen.

The Judgment

After three intense hearings, the Jodhpur High Court finally delivered its verdict. The court rejected the employees' appeal and ruled in favor of the company. The judge was in full agreement with Madhav's arguments. He stated that the company had acted within its legal rights and had followed the proper procedures in dealing with the appointments and dismissals of contingent workers.

Madhav stood in disbelief. His first courtroom experience, which had begun with anxiety and self-doubt, had ended in a resounding victory. The senior officials who had accompanied him to Jodhpur congratulated him on his success. This decision not only spared the company from a potentially costly outcome but also reinforced Madhav's reputation as a capable and resourceful leader.

A Moment of Triumph

Madhav couldn't help but feel a rush of pride. The victory was a significant milestone in his career—a testament to his perseverance, preparation, and legal insight. His ability to navigate a complex legal situation with little prior experience in the courtroom had earned him respect and admiration from his peers and superiors alike.

As he received congratulations from the company's top officials, Madhav realized that this was no ordinary victory. It wasn't just about winning the case—it was about proving to himself that he was ready to take on any challenge.

Conclusion: A New Chapter in Madhav's Career

Madhav's success in the Jodhpur High Court marked a defining moment in his career. He had faced his fears, stood before a judge, and argued a complex legal case without the safety net of experienced counsel.

His handling of the case earned him not just respect within the company but also opened new doors professionally. This legal victory was a clear testament to Madhav's ability to confront difficult situations, think on his feet, and remain calm under pressure.

More importantly, the case underscored the critical value of thorough preparation and a deep understanding of the law—especially in HR roles, where legal challenges often arise. Madhav had proven to himself and others that he was capable of navigating even the most daunting challenges.

As he returned to his office, Madhav knew this victory was just the beginning. More challenges would come, but after his experience in Jodhpur, he felt prepared to face whatever lay ahead with confidence and resolve.

"True success is not measured by the outcome, but by the courage to face the challenge, the resilience to stand firm, and the wisdom to turn every obstacle into an opportunity for growth."

22

The Picnic Adventure: A Day of Teamwork, Fun, and Memories

Madhav and Surendra, long-time friends and residents of ITI Township in Bengaluru, were feeling the weight of their busy routines. One evening, while enjoying tea in the township park, they discussed the idea of organizing a picnic. A simple day out of the hustle and bustle of daily life seemed like just what everyone needed. The weather in Bengaluru was pleasant, and the hills and greenery outside the city provided the perfect backdrop for a refreshing escape.

Madhav suggested that some senior members of the community should be included to make the journey even more interesting. Surendra agreed and proposed that everyone—family members, children, wives, and even the elderly—be invited. With excitement and a sense of adventure, the two friends began planning the event.

What they didn't realize was that organizing a picnic for a large group would require much more than enthusiasm.

Planning the Picnic

Madhav and Surendra began by reaching out to some senior colleagues in the township. Mr. Rao, an experienced manager and expert in organizing events, was the first to be approached. Mrs. Gupta, known for her vivacious nature, also expressed interest. As the idea spread, more families joined in, and the plan quickly transformed into a large-scale event.

It was decided that the picnic would be a one-day event, held outside Bengaluru in a picturesque location known for its lush greenery and tranquil lake. The first planning meeting took place at Surendra's house, where about ten people gathered, representing different families of the township. Over tea and breakfast, they discussed logistics — transportation, food, games, and activities. Each family agreed to bring home-cooked food to share, adding a personal touch to the picnic. Madhav suggested hiring a bus for the journey, and Mr. Rao immediately agreed.

As discussions progressed, it was decided that games like Antakshari and Tambola would be organized for everyone to enjoy. Music would play throughout the journey, creating a festive atmosphere. The group was buzzing with excitement, but soon, some disagreements began to emerge.

Objections and Challenges

While most of the group supported the plan, there were some objections. Mrs. Sharma, one of the senior members, expressed concern about the early start time. She pointed out that the elderly and children would struggle to get ready early in the morning. "Leaving at 5:30 AM is too early," she said.

Others voiced concerns about the funding for the bus and the seating arrangements to ensure everyone could travel comfortably. Mr. Verma, another senior resident, raised the issue of accommodating the elderly, who needed more space, and ensuring that children wouldn't be left unsupervised.

Despite these concerns, Madhav and Surendra were determined to make the picnic a success. They decided to hold another meeting at Madhav's residence to resolve the remaining issues.

Finalizing the Details

At the second meeting, the final details were ironed out. Adjustments were made to the schedule, ensuring a later departure time. Additional considerations were made for the elderly and children, and a more detailed plan for the bus seating was discussed. With everyone's concerns addressed, the excitement for the picnic grew even stronger.

Madhav and Surendra couldn't wait to see the plan come to life. With everyone on board and all the logistics in place, they knew that this picnic would be a day to remember—a day full of laughter, games, delicious food, and unforgettable memories.

The Final Meeting

Another important meeting took place at Madhav's house, with Mrs. Gupta taking the responsibility for organizing the meal. It was decided that each family should bring home-cooked food—something they personally enjoy preparing. This suggestion was warmly embraced by the group. However, a lively debate ensued regarding the seating arrangement on the bus. It was eventually agreed that seats would be allotted based on family needs. Elderly passengers would get the front seats for easier access, while families with small children would sit together in the middle of the bus. Surendra took charge of addressing the issue of timing, stressing the importance of leaving early to make the most of the day. If they left too late, there wouldn't be enough time to reach the picnic spot. After some convincing, everyone agreed, though reluctantly. The group also collected money for the bus fare, and the date for the picnic was finalized. The excitement was palpable, and even those who had previously expressed objections were now eagerly anticipating the trip.

The Picnic Day

The long-awaited morning of the picnic finally arrived. The bus, which was scheduled to reach Madhav's residence at 5:30 am, arrived late by 15 minutes. Gathering everyone proved more challenging than expected. Some families had overslept, others were still packing last-minute items, and a few were grumbling about the early start. When Mrs. Sharma boarded the bus, she remarked, "I knew 5:30 am was too early." By the time everyone was settled, it was already 7:30 am. As soon as the bus began its journey, the atmosphere lightened. The group's mood shifted to one of excitement. Madhav and Surendra spontaneously formed teams and started a game of Antakshari. The bus was filled with the sounds of old Hindi film songs. Soon, even the most reserved members of the group were joining in and singing along. There were a few who preferred not to participate, including the elderly Mr. Mehta, who decided to take a nap. He joked, leaning back in his seat, "I'm saving my energy for the picnic!"

Fun and Games

Upon reaching the picnic spot, the group was greeted by a beautiful, peaceful location—perfect for spending a day together. Blankets were spread out, and everyone began opening their tiffins. The variety of home-cooked food was incredible: aloo parathas, sandwiches, idlis, dosas, chutneys, sweets, and more. The sense of community was palpable, with people exchanging recipes and tasting each other's dishes. After the meal, the group split into smaller groups to enjoy different activities. Some played tambola, with Mrs. Gupta enthusiastically calling out the numbers, while others organized a game of cricket for the children. Meanwhile, the elders gathered under the shade of a large tree, enjoying the cool breeze and reminiscing about the good old days.

Moments of Tension

Despite the fun, there were a few moments of tension. Mrs. Sharma, who had previously been concerned about time, was now upset by how much time the group was spending on games. She grumbled that they should be exploring the area rather than just sitting around. Surendra, ever the peacemaker, stepped in to calm her down. "Don't worry," he reassured her, "there will be time for everything. Let's enjoy the moment." With his words, the tension dissolved, and the group returned to their leisurely activities, savoring the peaceful day together.

The Return Journey

The sun was setting as the group packed and prepared for the return journey. The day had been filled with laughter, games, and delicious food. The children were especially happy, spending hours playing and exploring the picnic spot. The return journey was quiet. People were satisfied despite being tired. Some slept on the bus, while others talked in low voices, reminiscing about the highlights of the day. Madhav and Surendra, sitting in front, were tired but happy. Despite challenges and objections along the way, they had a successful picnic. As soon as the bus reached the colony at 10 pm, everyone was ready to go home. The mood was upbeat, and the group exchanged goodbyes and thanks, also talking about planning the next picnic.

Reflection

Organizing the picnic was a learning experience for Madhav and Surendra. They faced many challenges, such as time issues, objections from some members, and the pressure of managing such a large group. They handled it all with patience and teamwork. The success of the picnic was a testament to the group's ability to work together despite their differences. The elder members of the group, like Mr. Mehta and Mrs. Sharma, enjoyed themselves as much as the children. Even those who had been hesitant to participate in the games had a great time. It was the coordination, team effort, and willingness to compromise that made the picnic a memorable and enjoyable experience for everyone involved. Madhav and Surendra were already thinking about the next outing. The joy of spending time with friends, family, and coworkers was worth all the effort.

"Success is not defined by how fast you reach your goal, but by how steadfastly you move forward, no matter the obstacles. Keep going, for every step brings you closer to your dreams."

23

Title: A Bold Decision: Madhav's Walk-in Recruitment Success

Madhav was sitting quietly at his desk. Over the past few weeks, I had been observing the pile of demand forms lying on his desk. Every department—engineering, marketing, IT, and operations—was in urgent need of manpower to keep pace with the company's growing workload. The pressure was mounting. The management had called for an immediate solution. The human resources department was responsible for finding candidates rapidly. Madhav had been promoted to the senior HR position a few days ago. He knew the work was important, and the deadline was limited.

The solution proposed by top management was unconventional. Following the normal recruitment process with formal applications and interview rounds was very time-consuming. Madhav decided to conduct walk-in interviews in Mumbai. It was a bold decision, and it was Madhav's responsibility to implement it. He had three colleagues in his team who would support him. The burden of work was heavy on his shoulders. An advertisement was placed in many leading newspapers. Candidates were invited to participate in the walk-in program. The aim was clear: to hire as many skilled people as possible in a single day, with the selection letters being issued by the same evening. The idea was to handle this process on a first-come, first-served basis.

Arriving in Mumbai

The day of the interview arrived, and Madhav flew to Mumbai with his three colleagues. As the plane touched down, Madhav couldn't shake the feeling of responsibility that lay ahead. Hosting walk-in interviews for over a hundred candidates was completely new for the company. Madhav felt the pressure to ensure that everything ran smoothly.

He had spent the past week reviewing company policies and human resources rules to ensure the recruitment process was in line with company standards. The conference room was simple, located in a hotel that was centrally positioned for easy access by the candidates. Upon arrival, the team set up the room: chairs and tables were arranged in neat rows. At the front of the room, Madhav placed a table where resumes would be reviewed, and candidates would be interviewed. The scheme was simple: candidates came with their biodata in hand. Madhav and his colleagues conducted one-on-one informal discussions with each candidate before making appointment decisions.

Madhav could not help but worry. This was different from the formal process he was accustomed to. Many apprehensions were arising in his mind, such as selecting the right candidates and being able to make recruitment decisions in real-time, among other concerns.

The Walk-In Begins

At 9 a.m., the doors opened, and the first crowd of candidates began arriving. They came in with their resumes, signed the register, and sat in the waiting room. By 10 a.m., the conference room was filled with more than 120 eager applicants. Everyone was waiting for the opportunity to create their own image. Madhav took a deep breath while looking at the room. He realized that his usual structured approach would not work here. There were too many people and too little time. Instead of formal interviews, Madhav and his colleagues thought of ways to save time. It was decided to approach the candidates casually with the aim of gathering as much information as possible from preliminary discussions. They knew they had to trust their instincts more than ever.

The interviews were conducted in a simple format. Informal talks were held. Instead of probing candidates with technical questions, Madhav and his colleagues gathered information about applicants' experiences and perspectives. The focus was on understanding how well the candidate would fit into the company culture. The candidates were seated in small groups. As soon as one interview was over, the next person was called forward. There were no formal appointments. The process was fluid and dynamic. This helped the team move things forward faster. By morning, Madhav felt the initial tension diminishing. One by one, the candidates sat down with their biodata in hand, and the discussions went on naturally. It was an informal process - resume in hand, a quick introduction, and then a discussion about the candidate's background and what they could bring to the table. Madhav had never taken an interview like this before. This was a new experiment. To his surprise, it worked. They found that candidates were more spontaneous and open. They could get a better understanding of who they really were. Breaking Tradition: On-the-Spot Offers

Over time, Madhav and his team talked to dozens of candidates. Some had strong technical skills but lacked experience. Others were a perfect cultural fit but needed training. After several hours of interviews, the team had a short list of candidates who met the company's needs. During the lunch break, Madhav brought up an idea that had been on his mind the whole morning. He told his colleagues that today they were doing things differently and that the offer letter could be issued that evening itself. His colleagues were surprised. Issuing offer letters on the same day as the interview had never happened before in the history of the company. Typically, this process involved further evaluation, approval from higher authorities, and days or even weeks of deliberation. Given the urgent need for manpower, Madhav felt that he could speed up the process. The candidates they had met were suitable. Departments needed people now. The team was satisfied with these interviews. The offer letters could be issued today. There was a pause in the room at this idea of Madhav's. The idea was bold, but his colleagues saw logic in it. After a brief discussion, they agreed. The candidates who were shortlisted were issued their offer letters on the spot.

The Final Selection

By the end of the day, Madhav and his team had narrowed down the pool of candidates to nine individuals. These were people who not only had the right skills but also demonstrated the right attitude and commitment. The company was looking for such a candidate. The selection process had been intensive but rewarding. Madhav felt a sense of accomplishment as he reviewed the list of final candidates. These were the engineers who had impressed the team during their informal interviews. The decision to forego the formalities had been successful, and Madhav felt confident that he had made the right choice. The candidates were waiting anxiously in the lobby, unaware of the outcome, while Madhav and his colleagues prepared the proposal papers. This was the first time in the company that offers would be given on the day of the interview itself. It was a significant departure from tradition. Madhav believed that this would save time and fill the urgent vacancies quickly.

Issuing the Offers

With offer letters in hand, Madhav gathered the final candidates in the conference room. He could see the nervous anticipation on their faces as they waited for the announcement. Madhav thanked everyone for coming that day. He further mentioned that he was very impressed by the quality of the candidates he had met. After careful consideration, the final selection had been made. He paused, letting the suspense build. Madhav then announced that offer letters were being issued to those who had been selected. A wave of surprised gasps filled the room. The candidates looked at each other in disbelief. Madhav smiled at their reactions. One by one, he and his colleagues called the successful candidates and handed them their offer letters. This was a proud moment for Madhav, knowing they had not only met the company's immediate staffing needs but had done so efficiently.

A New Era of Recruitment

As soon as the program ended, Madhav and his team packed up their things and got ready to go back to the hotel. Reflecting on that day, Madhav realized that he had achieved something remarkable. He had deviated from tradition and done something different. He had paved the way for a new, more efficient approach to recruitment. For Madhav, it had been a day of learning and growth. Initially hesitant and unsure whether the informal process would work, the success of the event showed him the importance of flexibility and quick decision-making. Madhav felt a sense of accomplishment. It wasn't just about filling vacancies; it was about taking bold steps to meet the company's needs in a new and innovative way. The walk-in interview had been a success. Madhav knew this would set a precedent for future recruitment drives.

"Great leaders don't fear opposition; they embrace it as a chance to prove their vision, build trust, and create lasting impact through perseverance and purpose."

24

Streamlining the Temporary Workforce: Madhav's Mission in Bangalore Plant

The Challenge at Hand

Madhav joined the bustling Bangalore plant of a renowned Public Sector Undertaking (PSU) with a clear mission: to implement major reforms and optimize its operations. The plant relied heavily on more than 859 temporary workers, originally hired under a scheme intended for a different purpose. Over time, these workers had become the backbone of the workforce, but their presence also created inefficiencies and sparked frustration among the management.

The root of the problem lay in the haphazard hiring process. Nepotism, bribery, and the influence of middle managers and union leaders had shaped much of the workforce. For Madhav, this presented a daunting challenge that required bold and strategic action.

The Initial Assessment

On his very first day, Madhav took a thorough walk through the workshop area, observing the deployment of temporary workers. He quickly noted inefficiencies:

- Some workers aimlessly wandered around.
- Others worked sluggishly or appeared disengaged.
- Many seemed unclear about their roles and responsibilities.

Conversations with line managers revealed deeper issues, such as poor communication and a lack of accountability. These problems were taking a toll on the plant's productivity.

Determined to uncover the full extent of the issue, Madhav held meetings with departmental heads to assess the actual manpower requirements. However, the situation was more complex than it seemed. Many managers had vested interests in maintaining the status quo:

- Some had hired workers through bribery or personal connections.
- Others feared that reducing the workforce would overburden their departments.

Despite these challenges, Madhav remained focused on his primary goal: to align the plant's operations with company regulations and ensure the judicious use of temporary personnel.

The Proposal: A Vision for Reform

After extensive research and consultations with honest departmental heads, Madhav developed a comprehensive proposal to optimize the workforce. His plan included:

1 **Manpower Assessment:** Evaluating the specific needs of each department to identify tasks that genuinely required additional personnel.
2 **Merit-Based Hiring:** Ensuring temporary employees were hired strictly based on merit and necessity, eliminating favoritism and bribery.
3 **Workforce Reduction:** Aiming to reduce the number of temporary workers by at least 70%.

This initiative promised significant savings for the company and a boost in operational efficiency. However, implementing such sweeping changes required the approval of the plant's head.

Support and Resistance

The plant's chief, an experienced and pragmatic leader, recognized the depth of the problem and supported Madhav's vision for reform. Yet, he also understood the potential fallout of such a drastic workforce reduction. Resistance was inevitable—from both managers with personal stakes in the current system and workers who feared job loss.

Madhav knew that executing these changes would be a delicate balancing act. His approach emphasized clear communication, transparency, and fairness to gain the trust of the workforce and management alike.

The Road Ahead

Madhav's mission was not just about cutting numbers but about transforming the plant into a more efficient and compliant operation. His efforts marked the beginning of a critical journey—one that promised to bring lasting change to the Bangalore plant while setting a benchmark for other PSU facilities across the country.

Challenges in Plant Operations: Union Politics and Communication Gaps

Opposition from Union Leaders

Union leaders, historically influential in plant operations, reacted angrily to Madhav's proposal for reforms. For years, these leaders had controlled hiring and firing, often leveraging their authority to secure jobs for their supporters or demand bribes for employment. Some leaders were deeply involved in corrupt practices, collaborating with line managers and local officials to maintain their dominance.

The workers these leaders represented formed the backbone of their power, and any reduction in workforce numbers posed a direct threat to their control. When Madhav attempted to discuss his proposal with the union leaders, he faced immediate resistance. The leaders initially refused to meet with him, fueling rumors of an impending conflict.

Fear and misinformation began to spread among the workers, with many suspecting that Madhav's plan was an attempt to undermine their job security altogether. The situation was further complicated by internal union politics, where rival factions vied for power. While some leaders fiercely opposed workforce reductions, others viewed the proposal as an opportunity to negotiate better terms for their members and improve their own standing within the union. These divisions made consensus nearly impossible, forcing Madhav to navigate the rivalries with extreme caution.

Poor Communication on the Shop Floor

The situation was exacerbated by a long-standing issue of poor communication between line managers and workshop staff. Temporary workers, in particular, felt insecure and uninformed about the plant's improvement plans. Many lacked a clear understanding of the proposal's intent, as line managers either neglected or deliberately avoided addressing their concerns.

This communication gap bred mistrust and low morale among employees, further fueling resistance to change. Recognizing the urgency of bridging this divide, Madhav took matters into his own hands. He began holding direct meetings with workers to explain the rationale behind the proposal.

Winning Trust Through Transparency

Madhav emphasized how the changes were designed to improve working conditions in the long run, addressing workers' fears and clarifying misunderstandings. While skepticism persisted among some employees, a few activists started to see the logic behind his plan. Madhav's direct approach marked a significant step toward rebuilding trust and fostering a more transparent relationship between management and workers.

Navigating the Road Ahead

Madhav's journey underscored the complex interplay between union politics, workforce dynamics, and leadership challenges. His efforts to balance the competing interests of union leaders, address worker insecurities, and improve communication highlighted the need for patience, strategy, and perseverance in driving meaningful change.

Nepotism and Bribery: A Hidden Crisis

During his investigation, Madhav uncovered alarming instances of nepotism and bribery that had infiltrated the plant's workforce. Many temporary workers were hired not based on merit but due to their connections with line managers or union leaders. Others secured their positions by paying bribes. This unethical practice had become disturbingly common.

Madhav discovered forged documents, discrepancies in employee qualifications, and evidence of payments made to middlemen acting as job brokers. This culture of corruption and favoritism severely impacted productivity. Workers who had paid bribes felt no genuine obligation to perform their duties diligently. They knew their positions were secured through unethical means. Similarly, those hired through favoritism relied on the protection of their superiors, making it nearly impossible to enforce discipline on the shop floor.

The Turning Point: A Vision for Change

Despite these challenges, Madhav was determined to bring about change. He recognized that addressing nepotism and corruption was crucial for improving the plant's productivity and work culture. His first step was to reduce the temporary workforce, which had become a breeding ground for unethical practices.

In a final effort to gain the support of union leaders, Madhav organized multiple meetings with them. This time, he focused on the long-term benefits of his proposal. Surprisingly, some union leaders, particularly those less entangled in corrupt practices, began to see the merit in his vision.

Madhav emphasized that reducing the number of temporary employees, if handled carefully, could enhance work culture and job security for the remaining workforce. Fewer, more qualified workers would lead to higher productivity and a more professional environment. Together with the union leaders, he devised an agreement:

1. **Letting Go of Unethical Hires:** Temporary employees hired through corrupt practices were dismissed.
2. **Retaining Valuable Talent:** Workers who performed well and were essential to operations were retained, with the possibility of permanent positions in the future.
3. **Improving Communication:** Madhav committed to fostering better communication between management and workers to ensure transparency about the reasons behind the changes.

The Outcome: A New Era of Efficiency

After weeks of negotiations, the proposal was approved by the plant's head. The workforce was reduced by 70%, leading to an immediate improvement in efficiency. The remaining employees, who had earned their positions through merit, were more motivated and committed to their roles. Productivity surged as the work culture shifted toward greater professionalism and accountability.

While resistance persisted from some union leaders and issues of corruption lingered in a few departments, the foundation for long-term reform had been laid. By optimizing manpower, enhancing communication, and addressing corruption, Madhav set the plant on a path to sustained efficiency and growth.

A Brighter Future

In the months that followed, the plant's performance continued to improve. Workers began to trust that management had their best interests at heart. Although union leaders remained divided, they acknowledged that the changes were benefiting both the company and its employees.

Madhav knew that the most challenging part of his mission was behind him. The plant's culture had transformed for the better, paving the way for a brighter and more secure future for its workforce.

"True change begins with courage—when you stand against corruption, inspire accountability, and build a foundation where merit thrives, progress becomes unstoppable."

25

A Promise Fulfilled: Madhav's Journey to a PhD

A Routine Email That Changed Everything

Madhav sat in his office, surrounded by the quiet hum of the marketing division. While sifting through emails, one caught his attention. It was a routine request for permission to pursue a PhD at Bengaluru University. The sender, Rajeev, was a diligent officer Madhav had always admired for his hard work.

As Madhav read the email, a flood of memories swept over him—a distant recollection buried under the weight of professional responsibilities and personal neglect. Something about Rajeev's request stirred an old, forgotten dream. Without hesitation, Madhav called Rajeev to discuss his plans. Rajeev spoke passionately about his ambitions, and his enthusiasm ignited a spark within Madhav.

A Pact with Friends and a Forgotten Promise

Madhav's mind traveled back to his days at IIT Kharagpur. He had once made a pact with his three closest friends—Amar, Dhiren, and Girish. They had vowed to pursue PhDs in their respective fields after securing jobs. It was a promise made with the optimism of youth and the thrill of chasing endless possibilities.

But life had its way of diverting paths. Amid the pressures of a high-ranking job and the responsibilities of daily life, Madhav had not only forgotten the pact but also a promise he had made to his late father—to never stop learning and growing.

Rajeev's email acted as a wake-up call. It rekindled a dormant desire within Madhav. Could this be his second chance to fulfill those long-lost dreams?

Taking the Leap

Fueled by a newfound determination, Madhav immediately downloaded the PhD application form from Bengaluru University's website. He meticulously filled out the form, gathered the necessary documents, and submitted his application for approval.

Though excitement coursed through him, Madhav knew the journey ahead would be fraught with challenges. As Chief Manager of Human Resources, his role was demanding, and balancing work with academic pursuits would require immense effort.

The Preparation Begins

With his division head's approval secured, Madhav joined forces with Rajeev to prepare for the PhD entrance exam. Having been out of academia for years, Madhav felt a mix of excitement and apprehension. He had no idea what to expect and often found himself overwhelmed during study sessions.

Yet, Rajeev's shared enthusiasm became a source of motivation. Together, they navigated their uncertainties, fueled by a common goal: to succeed.

Facing the Entrance Exam

As the exam day approached, Madhav's nerves began to fray. Doubts crept into his mind.

What if I fail?

What if I can't manage the workload?

What if I've forgotten how to study?

When Madhav arrived at the exam center, he was greeted by a sea of over 450 candidates, most of them young students brimming with energy. Sitting among them, he couldn't help but feel like a relic of a different era.

But as he took his seat, Madhav reminded himself of his purpose. This wasn't just about reclaiming a forgotten dream; it was about proving to himself that age, time, and challenges were no barriers to growth.

A Journey Rekindle

The exam hall buzzed with youthful energy, and Madhav found himself oddly inspired. While the process was intimidating, it also felt like a reclaiming of something precious—a promise to himself, his friends, and his late father.

Madhav realized this was more than just an academic pursuit. It was a journey of rediscovery, resilience, and fulfilling the promises of a life well-lived.

Madhav's Moment of Triumph

When the results were announced, Madhav couldn't believe his eyes. His name was at the top of the list. He kept looking at it over and over again, and with each glance, the reality sank in—he had topped the exam. It was a moment of sheer disbelief and uncontainable happiness. But this was just the beginning. The road ahead was long, and this was only the first step. Madhav knew that to complete his PhD would require years of hard work, sleepless nights, and unwavering dedication to his goal.

The Journey Begins

Madhav enrolled in his PhD program, inspired and motivated by the memories of his friends—Amar, Dhiren, and Girish. Each of them had completed their own PhD, and their journeys served as a beacon of hope for him.

Amar had completed his PhD in 2000, taking six years of dedicated effort. Dhiren, after four and a half years of intense work, had finished his studies in 2002. Girish had recently completed his PhD in 2018, after five years of hard work. Now, in his fifty-fourth year, Madhav understood the challenges ahead. It would not be easy.

The Struggle to Balance Work and Study

Madhav was fully aware of the challenges that lay ahead. As he juggled his professional commitments and academic responsibilities, he realized just how difficult it was to balance work with his research. The first few months were filled with doubt and confusion. Managing daily meetings, handling HR duties, and addressing employee complaints drained him. By the end of each day, he was mentally exhausted, and often, when he sat down to work on his thesis, his mind went blank. The days blurred into nights, and exhaustion became a constant companion.

In moments of despair, Madhav questioned whether he had taken on too much responsibility. But he never gave up. He had made promises—to his father, to his friends, and most importantly, to himself. He reminded himself of the commitments he had made years ago, when each of his friends had overcome their own struggles to earn their PhDs. If they could do it, so could he. It was the determination to keep pushing forward, no matter how difficult things got.

The Power of Promise and Perseverance

These promises gave Madhav strength in his darkest moments. There were times when his research seemed like an insurmountable mountain. Deadlines loomed large, and progress was agonizingly slow. He had to revisit topics he hadn't touched in years, rethink old principles, and learn new ones. The academic world had evolved since his student days, and he needed to adapt.

But with each challenge came a new lesson. Each obstacle became an opportunity to grow, and each setback fueled his determination. Madhav's journey was not just about academic success; it was about perseverance, resilience, and the relentless pursuit of a dream that had always seemed just out of reach.

The Journey of Perseverance: Madhav's PhD Story

The Beginning of the Struggle

Learning required extra effort, but Madhav felt a new sense of purpose as each paper was reviewed. Determined to succeed, he created a strict schedule to manage his time effectively. His working hours were dedicated to professional duties, while late evenings and weekends were devoted entirely to his research. Social activities were abandoned, and sleep became a luxury. Madhav kept moving forward, day and night, gradually completing the immense task before him.

Family Support: A Pillar of Strength

Madhav's family, witnessing his dedication, extended their unwavering support. In moments of doubt, they offered encouragement that helped him keep going. As the years passed, Madhav's PhD became more than just an academic pursuit; it became a symbol of his perseverance and his ability to overcome any obstacle.

Time Management and Personal Growth

Through this journey, Madhav learned invaluable lessons. He discovered how to prioritize tasks, manage his time better, and remain focused despite the chaos surrounding him. Each challenge he faced only strengthened his resolve. Patience and determination became his guiding principles, and with each passing year, he grew not only as a researcher but also as a human being.

The Long Road to Completion

By the time Madhav was nearing the completion of his PhD, he had spent seven long years working on his thesis. The process was far from smooth, but each setback taught him something valuable. Over these seven years, Madhav learned the importance of flexibility and how to keep promises even when the obstacles seemed insurmountable.

The Reward of Perseverance

The journey was undeniably difficult, but it was also immensely rewarding. In 2022, Madhav finally submitted his complete thesis and awaited the final results. A sense of peace spread through his mind, for regardless of the outcome, Madhav had fulfilled a promise he had made to himself and his father many years ago.

The Emotional Triumph

When the news came that he had successfully completed his PhD, Madhav was overwhelmed with emotion. It wasn't just a degree; it was the culmination of years of hard work, sleepless nights, and tireless determination. This achievement was a testament to his perseverance and resilience.

A Legacy of Strength and Determination

Madhav's PhD journey wasn't merely about academic achievement; it was a profound lesson in the power of perseverance, the importance of keeping promises, and the fulfillment that comes from overcoming adversity. Reflecting on his journey, Madhav felt a deep sense of satisfaction. He had not only earned his PhD but had also proven to himself that no dream is too big for someone willing to give everything for it.

"***True success isn't measured by the destination, but by the perseverance, sacrifices, and growth along the journey. Keep your promises, embrace every challenge, and never underestimate the power of relentless determination.***"